SELF

The Vast World
Behind Your Words

JOEL B. KIMMEL

IngramSpark Publishing   www.ingramspark.com

CONTENTS

PROLOGUE

ACCESSING THE VAST WORLD BEHIND YOUR WORDS

I have always been fascinated by the world we live in and that our lives are solely connected by our ability to effectively share our thoughts and interpretations with one another.

The more that ability allows us to see our interpretation of the moment from outside ourselves, the greater our opportunity to live a more peaceful life. There is something magical in a "moment" when we are sharing our experience with another; we bring our two worlds closer together just by listening to what is unfolding in the other, rather than listening for who is right or wrong.

I have been asked by a large number of our clients and friends to write a book that would allow readers to live from this more peaceful and authentic place in their world. They have seen the shifts that have taken place in their lives from the work we have done together, and they want their friends to have this same kind of opportunity.

One of the puzzles about having that Shift to a more authentic way of living is that it doesn't happen in the same way we have lived our lives in the past. We have been taught to "Do something different" to make something change. If that doesn't work then "Do something else

DON'T "READ" THIS BOOK

We usually read books of this kind from the outside–looking inward. Instead I want to invite you to read this book as though you were its author, crafting the message as you go along.

This shift in perspective may seem simple, yet it can be very powerful. This book is intentionally written using stories, examples, analogies, metaphors, and suggested actions to support you in having a personal experience of what you are learning as you read.

My goal is for you to place yourself front and center inside this huge conversation about "the Self that you don't know yourself to be." My hope is that you will experience the flow of what is being said and allow the impact of the message to enter your everyday life.

different", and eventually something will change.

The question is, is it the change you wanted in the first place, or did you find yourself making it because it was close enough to what you thought you wanted?

I suggest that there is another avenue to follow, one that facilitates that Shift, one that can reveal a new way of Being that is in alignment with the world we are living in. That path naturally leads us to who we can see ourselves Being, and that will allow us to make the contribution that we came here to make.

While reading this book, I invite you to take your time to see the shifts that are taking place, the new perspectives that are appearing and the new actions you see yourself taking that will have you living a more peaceful and engaged life. As you delve into the pages, I believe that you too will start to see a natural way of living in your world. Your language may begin to shift and along with it, your experience of your brilliance.

Additionally I want to thank my wife, Judy, who has been an equal partner in this collaboration. Although the book is written through my eyes, she has played a strategic and foundational role in finding just the right words, guiding me through our writing process and reminding me of that long forgotten story to reinforce a challenging distinction.

One final thought: We're all in this game called life—together. We might have different uniforms, paths, and points of view, but we're all heading toward and striving to experience a life well lived. It's my goal that this book allows you to see ways we can join together to support each other with plenty of room for cooperation, imagination, alignment, and success.

Please feel free to email us with your discoveries, new ways of being, and any moments that are "good enough to be true." It is a joy that you are reading this book and that we can have a meaningful relationship without having to meet face to face. Isn't this a magical world we are already living in?

Enjoy, Joel

CHAPTER 1:
LIVING IN LANGUAGE

"Traveler, there is no path. Paths are made by walking."

A. MACHADO

When I was a kid, iconic cowboy hero Hopalong Cassidy appeared on our black-and-white TV every Sunday morning. He was so real to me that I could almost taste the dust as his horse galloped by.

Hopalong always wore a white hat, a black shirt, and of course holstered a gun. The thing is—he never shot anybody. Instead, he scared the bad guys away and found a way to rescue the people who needed his help.

One warm morning in August, after watching The Hopalong Cassidy Show, I ran to my toy box, grabbed my black holster, silver cap gun, and white hat, and went outside. With the holster securely buckled to my hip, I climbed up into my favorite apple tree and looked over the lush landscape of our eastside neighborhood in Cleveland with its rolling hills, white picket fences, and friendly neighbors. Sitting there I thought, "Wouldn't it be great to be just like Hopalong, and help people get what they wanted out of life?"

I had forgotten all about that until one day recently, when a client asked where my work began. In that moment, I realized it all started with Hopalong Cassidy. But instead of rescuing people from bad guys so they can have the lives they want, I help them overcome their own internal voices and self-defeating thoughts—so they can use their own brilliance to have the lives they want.

And my weapon is not a holstered gun. It's language.

WORDS SHAPE REALITY

Communication and language are more than just the words people speak. While the words are important, there's a whole other world happening behind them.

The words we speak, questions we ponder, and language we listen to shape our perceptions of the world—both in that immediate moment and over the course of our lifetime.

For example, if you say you hate broccoli, the next time you see broccoli, no matter how it is prepared, your first thought will be I hate broccoli. If you decide you don't like a particular person, the next time you see them, you'll find yourself reflexively thinking, I don't like you. If you tell yourself you can't do something, you'll continue believing you can't, even if in reality you have the skill and/or talent to do it.

The impact of our words, and what's happening behind those words, doesn't just shape how we see ourselves; it shapes how other people see us as well. I learned that lesson when I was six years old.

My parents were having a cocktail party, and I was sitting on the stairs watching the guests as they came into the living room. One guest said, "Hello," and the room lit up. Everyone called back, "Hey! How are you?" and they really engaged with that person. Then someone else walked in and said, "Hello," and nothing happened.

I couldn't understand it. I thought it was the words that had elicited a reaction, but there was obviously more to it than that. As I watched different people interact throughout the evening, I noticed that there was more going on than just what the guests were saying.

That experience fascinated me. I pondered in my own childish thoughts on how communication worked. Ever since that party, I've been an observer of the dynamics of language and the power it has in our lives.

"The words we speak, questions we ponder, and language we listen to shape our perceptions of the world—both in that immediate moment and over the course of our lifetime."

I was fortunate enough to major in interpersonal and mass media communication in college, thanks to funding from the GI Bill. My Self education in the domain of language continued.

I'd been drafted into the Army, gone to Vietnam, and come home mostly in one piece. After a tour in Norfolk, Virginia, training Vietnamese helicopter crew chiefs and pilots, I was transferred to Nuremberg, Germany, where I spent a few months in a trucking outfit, counting nuts and bolts. In retrospect I am clear language has a lot to do with a person's future; often it's casual comments that may lead to a new opportunity.

Back to counting nuts and bolts. For some reason that is still not entirely clear to me, I was assigned the responsibility of running that trucking line, which meant fixing all the broken trucks. When I arrived on base the first bright Monday in September, my department was in shambles, my men, former Vietnam GIs, were counting the days until they were discharged. No one wanted to be there; no one had any incentive to change the status quo. What happened next, however, was life altering.

I was speaking to my commanding officer the very next day, and for some reason we were talking about skiing. He mentioned that his kids were passionately interested in learning how to ski. At that moment, I had an epiphany and blurted out that I was a former ski instructor and would be thrilled to coach his entire family, if I was able to get reassigned to the Armed Forces Recreation Center in Garmisch. I knew this was a long shot, but I thought I'd put myself out there.

A week later my commanding officer ventured back to the trucking department and made me the offer of a lifetime. Little did I know the powerful changes that would occur from accepting that request.

It appeared that there would be an inspector general review of the base in a few weeks, and he presented his challenge: If my unit could pass the inspection with flying colors—a huge feat considering where my men and the department were at the time—he would

"There's a vast other world happening behind your words."

support me in getting reassigned to run the ski school in Garmisch, and I would give his family ski lessons when they were in Bavaria. With no hesitation I gave my word, a resounding "Yes." Trucking would pass the IG with flying colors. Oh, and by the way, if we didn't pass the inspection, I would spend the rest of my time in the Army fixing trucks.

Later that evening, back in my barracks, I reviewed my situation. "Okay, that was a bold promise I made." I'd given my word. My future and my new wife's future were at stake. My current quality of my life as I knew it was on the line.

The next morning, I shot out of bed and arrived at the trucking depot bright and early. As usual, the place was a mess . . . truck parts scattered everywhere, nuts and bolts in huge bins, mixed up and unaccounted for. Not knowing what my next move would be, I sat down in front of a bin of large four-inch screws, dumped them on a table, and started counting, sorting out the mismatched sizes and types.

By midday I had one barrel done—4,446 four-inch screws sorted and accounted for. I placed a big sign on the top asking everyone in the unit not to disturb that bin. On I went to the next barrel. Initially the rest of the men ignored my efforts, then started to tease and eventually began to ask questions. "What are you doing, Kimmel? Are you trying to impress the other officers?" and on it went.

I responded to their ribbing saying that in fact there was nothing else to do and it was sort of a good game to play with myself. How many bins could I count in one day?

One by one, a man would join me, counting and joking all the way until pretty soon, the entire unit got involved, counting, cleaning, sorting and, labeling. It took three weeks to get the job done just in time for the IG inspection. Our area of the company was the only one that passed with flying colors. In the end, my unit gained a certain pride and dignity in their work; our effort was amazing to observe.

I was moved by everyone's commitment and even more moved by the men and the outcome we had produced. It was also remarkable to realize that those actions were ultimately the outcome of a strong intention and one word I had uttered, my "Yes" to the commanding officer.

The next morning I was called down to the commanding officer's office for a meeting. I walked in and saw him sitting behind his desk with a grin. As he looked up at me, he saluted and congratulated me for the excellent job my department had done in preparing

"It's interesting in life when you can allow others to join in on your game."

for the IG's tour. I thanked him and said it took the whole team to get the job done. He then picked up a group of papers and said, "'These are your orders to go to Garmisch to try out for the ski patrol. If you make it, my family will see your there."

I smiled and said I would be looking forward to seeing them there anytime.

LIFE LESSONS THE HARD WAY

About a month later, in the late fall, I was transferred to Garmisch, Germany. My assignment was to help run the Armed Forces Recreation Center in the Alps as part of the ski patrol and ski schools. I was going to have to try out, and if I made it, Judy and I would spend the next six months skiing in the Alps. The tryouts went by very fast, and by the end of the week I had been accepted to be on the team.

What a gift. We were living in one of the most beautiful places on the planet, and my job was to take care of the military families who would be coming there for their R&R.

One glorious, sparkling day on the Zugspitze, I was racing downhill in the glistening snow. At that moment, I was living in a postcard. The next moment, I was on the brink of death.

In those days we didn't wear ski helmets. My ski patrol partner was just ahead of me. We were almost at the bottom of the mountain, on a narrow trail between fir trees, skiing extremely fast, when I came around the corner and caught an outside edge. I fell head over heels and slid directly into the end of a log cabin.

The accident involved a dramatic, severe impact. I broke my back and my neck, fractured my skull, and was paralyzed. I spent the next seven months in various hospitals in Germany and back in the States, recovering. Part of that time, I was completely paralyzed. All I could do was stare at the ceiling. My vision was like a kaleidoscope because of the swelling in my head.

For the most part during those months, I was alone with my thoughts. People would come to see me and stand beside the bed, just out of view. I remember asking them to move up toward my head so I could see their outlines. Language and tunnel vision were all I had.

The reports from the doctors were crushing to my family. They said I would probably never walk again and that I should be glad I was alive. Much later, when I heard the diagnosis, I looked at Judy and said to her that if I was going to be a quadriplegic, I thought we should get divorced. When she asked why, I told her I was unwilling to have her life be about dragging me around and that she deserved more than that.

She then looked at me with deep compassion, held my hand, and said, "Why don't we talk about that when we need to?"

We never have had that conversation, and now, after forty-eight years of marriage, I am thankful we probably never will.

Eventually, the doctors determined that I would be medically evacuated to the Army trauma hospital in Landstuhl, just outside of Frankfort, and then eventually sent on to Walter Reed Hospital in Washington D.C.

I will never forget the cold, gray day I was wheeled out on a stretcher to the middle of a field. The Army had scheduled a Huey helicopter to take me to the first stop of my journey home. I was still paralyzed and still having difficulty seeing. They had bundled me up in those big, feather-filled comforters and had me lying in the sunshine waiting for the helicopter to arrive. Judy was there with her mother; they would drive in our old VW van to meet me at the next hospital.

The Huey landed, and as they slid my stretcher into the ship, I felt someone tapping me on the shoulder. I looked up and saw the commanding officer from my old trucking outfit in Nuremberg. He had asked permission to fly me to Landstuhl. I was moved to tears.

I later learned he had been a helicopter pilot in Vietnam and liked running the trucking unit about as much as I did.

The trip was a blur. We landed an hour later, and as they were taking me off the ship they paused. That someone familiar put his hand on my shoulder. My pilot for this flight, my former commanding officer, said, "Joel, thank you for taking the time to teach my family how to ski. They loved every moment of it."

I nodded a thank you to him for the opportunity.

He then said, "Take care of yourself, Soldier. Everything will be fine."

If I could have saluted, I would have. Instead I winked at him and nodded I would.

Time passed painfully and slowly, and eventually I arrived stateside at Walter Reed, my home base for rehab. I was processed in, and a young physical therapist came to my room and took me to the PT ward. She pulled me onto the mats, and as I lay there on my back, she asked me to roll over. Needless to say I could only slightly move my head, trying to use it to say no.

She said that was fine, not to worry, then asked me if I liked to swim. I nodded "Sure," and she took me off to the physical therapy pool, put floaties on me so I wouldn't tip over, and asked the guys in the pool to make sure I didn't end up head down. I floated in the water like that day after day, and eventually the pain went away and things started to shift.

We moved on from there to hours of basic, infantile mat work in the physical therapy room, and then she finally got me up, put me between some handrails, and commanded, "Walk to me, Soldier."

I struggled to her, stepping out as best I could, dragging my right leg, and collapsed into a wheelchair. She held my face between her hands, kissed me on the forehead, and said, "You'll be fine."

I've never seen her again, but I've never forgotten her or her magic words.

Out of that trauma experience, I started looking a little deeper into the meaning of life and began to ponder how we all "live in language." When you are paralyzed, that's all you have, your inner thoughts. There was lots of time to ponder life during that initial period of mental isolation as I lay on my hospital bed staring at the ceiling tiles. Gradually, my ability to communicate by speaking came back.

Spending seven months recovering made a profound distinction simple for me to see: The language we use—in our thoughts and conversations—shapes who we are Being. And who we are Being shapes the world around us.

If you get up in the morning and you're grumpy, the day will be grumpy, and chances are everyone around you will be grumpy as well. If you are in a good mood, the day will most likely seem good and others around you happy.

"It is the language we live in that shapes how we see and experience the world around us."

One of my major purposes in writing this book is to allow others to understand these principles:

- Who you are Being in the world at any moment creates the contribution you make to the world.
- When you allow yourself to see who you are Being in the world at any moment, you discover your life aligning with who you would like to be, and you can then stop focusing on what you like or don't like.
- When you start seeing new ways of Being, you get a new interpretation of yourself. It's a shift that starts with the way we speak and listen: the language of life.
- When you start to perceive and observe yourself and your language, the way you speak can set you free.

All of these principles can liberate you from most challenging situations—both the internal struggles and the conflicts with others.

When you start to perceive and observe yourself and your language, the way you speak can set you free. It can liberate you from most challenging situations—both the internal struggles and conflicts with others.

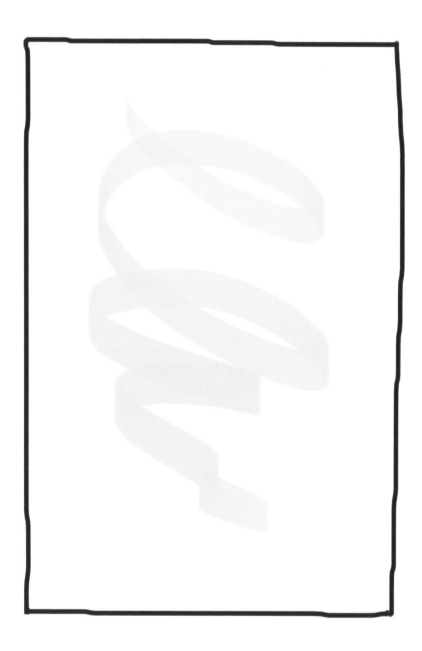

DISCOVERING A NEW WAY OF LIVING OUTSIDE OUR MATRIX

In the movie The Matrix, life is dramatically revealed to be without much joy: controlled by technology, lacking in self-expression, and driven by the need to survive. In some ways, our modern life today reflects some of these same themes—minus the ability to plug our heads into a computer and travel to other dimensions, of course.

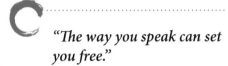

"The way you speak can set you free."

It is my goal to liberate us from this societally contrived model. The result doesn't take work; it just takes an awareness to see that we are already surrounded by exactly what we need to live the life of our choice.

My contribution toward this expanded awareness is by being an Ontological Design Coach. Ontology is the study of the existence of things. My specific area of study is how we live in language.

People come to me at different moments in their lives. All of them are looking for new ways to live in language that allow the world to occur in alignment with who they see themselves Being, who they see their kids Being, how they see their family Being, and how they see the world Being.

Once you have that vision for how things could be, you can see how your contributions will allow that vision to unfold, without a lot of effort and challenge.

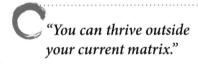

"You can thrive outside your current matrix."

In seeing your full possibilities and this natural way of living in your world, another benefit emerges. Through language, you can change how you experience not only your gifts, but the gifts of everyone around you. We're all here together in the same game. The question is, how can we live together in a way that nurtures each other and allows plenty of space for imagination and success?

QUESTIONS TO PONDER

1. What drew you to pick up this book and begin reading it? If you could have those ideas realized, what could you possibly do differently and what would your life look like?

2. After reading the first chapter of this book, what new benefits do you see you could gain from reading it?

3. What new interpretations do you have about the power of language and its ability to reshape your life as you speak?

CHAPTER 2:
BEING VS. DOING

"Tomorrow to fresh woods, and pastures new."

JOHN MILTON

People often come to me in transition—when they're retiring, between jobs, changing careers, moving, or ending relationships. I always ask them: "What questions are you asking yourself?"

The most common answer: "I'm asking myself what I should DO next."

The problem is that this is usually the wrong question. When we are trying to determine what's next for our lives, the better question to ask ourselves might be "Who can I see myself Being that would allow me to make the contributions I came here to make, for myself and those around me? What would that look like?"

Now, that's something to ponder.

A thirty-something friend of mine named James had started a website with a close friend. The company was becoming well known in the fashion industry, but the more successful the business became, the more strain it put on the friendship, and the venture started to break down.

James spent a year or two trying to scotch tape operations back together. He didn't want to throw in the towel since he had spent years investing his heart and soul into the site.

So, one lovely spring afternoon, he came to see me, hoping I could help resolve his career predicament. The sun was shining and the air was quiet as we sat in my office looking out at the verdant Marin Hills. I asked what questions he was asking himself, and he provided the typical answers: What should I DO next? How should I DO that? When should I DO that?

I suggested he reframe his questions from Doing to Being.

He took these questions on with a passion and started listening to what he was hearing. Within three months, he had completed his business relationship with his partner, financially and professionally, and they remained friends. He'd also landed two consulting jobs, which led him to a management position at a one-for-one company—a visionary company with a focus on contribution and profit. Now we know we can do both!

To this day, James says he probably would never have thought to take all the actions he took if he had simply been determined to DO something. When he started asking who he could see himself being that would allow him to make the contribution he would like to make, the world began offering a variety of intriguing possibilities. He saw who he could SEE himself Being—someone who loved to work, loved to be engaged in the world, and loved to take care of people. When those three passions emerged in his awareness, all the world started to reveal itself.

Throughout this book, I'll share many stories that represent this phenomenon—stories from high-level executives, world-renowned companies, politicians, friends, and artists, all of them seeking to define the next chapter of their lives or the next phase of their businesses.

"The universe has a better idea of where we fit into the grander scheme than we ever will."

My suggestion to all of them (and to you) is: "Why don't you take the next 30 days and instead of figuring out what to do in your next 50 years, see what the world offers you?"

The universe has a better idea of where we fit into the grander scheme than we ever will. So instead of trying to figure it out, why don't we observe what is being offered and get on board with that?

LIVING IN TWO DOMAINS

Both the Being and Doing domains are extremely valuable, because we're always trafficking back and forth between them. They are each essential to our lives.

In the Doing domain, you plan and take action. You make "to-do" lists for projects, outcomes, and production. We all need to do that.

In the Being domain, who we are Being creates the quality of our lives. Let's say I get up in the morning, and I've planned to go sailing that day. That's what I intend to be Doing. But it's raining outside. All of a sudden, I feel grumpy; I say I'm in a grumpy mood, and more than likely my entire

WHO CAN YOU SEE YOURSELF BEING OVER THE NEXT 50 YEARS?

I have a client who is a very senior leader in the financial world and as a result was contacted by the Presidential Financial Advisory Board and asked to serve, an honor extended to only a small handful of her colleagues.

The funny thing is that had you spoken to her just a year or two ago about how she saw her future, she never would have imagined that possibility. It was not until she embraced who she could see herself Being–that her path came into focus.

Today, in addition to her high-powered job as a financial executive, she's traveling around the world as a former member of the Presidential Advisory Board, doing exactly what she envisioned–educating youth about financial literacy.

As for the pressures of her work and the time constraints they create? She simply said, "I have all the time in the world because it's who I can see myself Being over the next 50 years that counts."

day will have a grumpy overtone. And because grumpy people attract grumpy people, I'll spend my day in the company of unhappy fellow humans.

The next day I get up and it's still pouring rain, but I say, "I feel great." The next thing I know, a parking space is right where I need it, and everyone around me seems to be in a good mood. Who I'm Being—happy verses grumpy—determines the way the world occurs for me.

It really is that simple. I can't DO anything about the rain. But I can change who I am BEING.

The Being domain lives in choice and language and has the power to take you outside the societal matrix. The words you choose set the tone for every moment and provide context for your life.

"'Being' creates the quality of our lives."

The Doing domain also involves language—words that can lead to a lot of worrying: Did I get it done right? Is this the right thing to have done? Did I say the right thing? Will I be able to get this done? If I do this, will bad things happen?

Doing is vital to our lives, but if we spend all our time there—if we get caught in the Doing trap—we can lose sight of glorious possibilities of Being as they fly by.

Once you start to have a clear vision—where you can see yourself Being—the Doing actions and language wrap around your vision. The world will bring you only the things you need to do to fulfill who you want to be.

"It is who you're Being while you're doing what you're doing that determines the quality of your life."

Not long ago, I met with the president of a large division of a leading U.S. bank. For about an hour, he told me what he wanted to have happen in his life, which is different from what he wanted to do. What we want to "have happen" is in the Being domain. What we want to "do in our lives" is in the Doing domain.

Six months later, I met with him again, and every major thing he had wanted to "have happen" had happened— from lecturing at some premiere universities, to writing a book about his new interpretation of the impact of wealth, to having all his relationships work better. One of his most cherished outcomes involved his son, who had asked to attend a more academically challenging school. He was astounded (and pleased) since previously, his son had not expressed any interest in academics.

"I don't understand how this works," he said.

"Don't worry about that," I told him. "Just be thankful it's happening and keep following your heart, and the Being side, and your life will continue to unfold in amazing and unexpected ways."

Another client of mine, Richard, the founder of a successful insurance firm,

TEACH YOUR CHILDREN WELL—TO BE

I've been married to my extraordinary wife, Judy, for forty-eight years. She is the best person I know—in fact, from my point of view, she may be the best person on the planet. And we are lucky to have two very successful, powerful, and caring daughters whom we adore. That is who I have always wanted to Be, someone with a great marriage, whose children have lives compatible with who they can see themselves Being. Very rarely when they were growing up did we ever have more than three rules for them:

- "Don't hurt yourself (or anyone else)."
- "Do your homework."
- Be where you tell us you're going to be."

They had just a few important instructions to live by, with clear consequences if they broke them. Since they knew that they were ultimately responsible for the quality of their lives, they had the opportunity to design their Being. Additionally, and just as importantly, that is also who my Being intended them to be.

READ THIS BOOK AS BEING, NOT DOING

Since I discovered that we live in a two-domain world (Doing and Being), there has been a shift in how I see my life and the people around me. I experience that the Doing side calls for actions to change things and the Being side calls for awareness and trust that what is happening is the right thing to be occurring or it wouldn't be taking place.

Both dance together, and which domain is leading determines the mood we find ourselves in. I suggest that when we allow ourselves to be led by the Being, there is a more peaceful experience and an engaged quality of living, than when we spend our time just Doing things.

I wrote this book with the intention that you, the reader, will become the observer of how these shifts unfold naturally. Unlike most books you read, this one happens in the "Being" side of life.

This book is written directly to you and is intended to allow you to live the life you have always known you could live. Not to prove anything to anyone, but to give you the opportunity to just be the you you have always known yourself to be.

put it like this:

"Looking back I realize that I judged and measured my life by what I was accomplishing. I also judged myself on how I could make everything better for others, regardless of the toll it took on my body, my spirit, or my potential. Life was a constant swirl of 'shoulds' and 'oughts.' I was unaware of my 'Being.'

"Once I started to take steps to acknowledge the results that come from 'Being,' the stress, and the loneliness, were overcome with who I always was inside, not acting under a self-imposed obligation to others. Peace came from the realization that my identity does not come from my work, but my work comes from my identity."

THE RIGHT QUESTION MAKES ALL THE DIFFERENCE

At the end of each chapter, you will find two groupings of questions: one focused on asking Doing types of questions and the other on asking Being questions.

The "Doing" questions live in our world of action. "If I do this, will I get that?" Or "If I don't do this, will it prevent that from happening?" Or "What if I do this to see what happens and then see what next actions I could take to accomplish the task?" All involve actions causing something to happen in a moment of the future.

The "Being" questions live in the world of awareness and discovery. Being questions might be something like "What would my life look like if I allowed my greatness to shine?" Or "If I was going to make a contribution to those around me, what would it look like and who could I see myself being while expressing that contribution?" Or "What would it look like to have a meaningful relationship that would allow both of us to thrive, both individually and together?"

As you may discover while reading the book, Being questions present the opportunity to open yourself to new interpretations, ideas, and ways of being, both for yourself and your world.

READ THIS BOOK AS BEING, NOT DOING (CONT.)

This is a book of discovery, where the mantra is "Isn't that interesting?" rather than one of assessment, agreeing or disagreeing with what you read. In the Being world, all things can be seen as possible if we allow ourselves to look newly at the way in which we are living.

QUESTIONS TO PONDER

Doing side of life:

1. Write down the five things you do that limit your ability to Be more present.

2. If you were more present to Being who you know you are, rather than just Doing what you're doing, what would that look like—to you and those around you?

Being side of life:

1. What new ways of Being do you see now that were not visible before, and what new actions can you see yourself beginning to take naturally?

2. Are you beginning to see how other people's worlds seem to fit with the types of words they are using and saying? If so, where do you see that same phenomenon happening in your personal life?

CHAPTER 3:
IT'S NOT ABOUT THE WORDS

"Everything that exists exists because someone is speaking."

DR. FERNANDO FLORES

As you live each day and encounter personal challenges, if you are lucky, you'll have a powerful, pivotal person step into your life. Dr Fernando Flores was that person for me.

Born in Talca, Chile, Fernando became finance minister in the government of Chilean president Salvador Allende. When Allende was overthrown by the military coup of General Augusto Pinochet, he sent Fernando, a gifted negotiator, to speak with Pinochet.

General Pinochet's regime held Fernando prisoner from 1973 to 1976. While being subjected to prolonged, systematic psychological torture, Fernando continued observing what distinguishes human beings from other living creatures.

During that period, he came up with various founding principles of being human. One was that the only thing that differentiates us as human beings is the ability to coordinate actions by making requests and promises. If we couldn't do so, we'd spend our lives looking for food like most every other animal on the planet.

After being extracted from Chile by Amnesty International, Fernando and his wife moved to Berkeley, California, where he began a teaching fellowship, essentially reintroducing the behavioral science of Ontology into the academic domain. Out of that discipline, he initiated his Communication for Action, commitment-based management work.

That's when I began to work with Fernando as his aid, spending almost every day with him. One morning not too far into the job, he said in his charming broken English, "Joel, I have offer for you. I offer to return you to that which is to be a fully human being. You accept?"

Hell, yes, I thought. The guy's a genius.

When I told him I accepted, he said, "Fine. I need to talk to Judy, your wife. Bring her here, and I need her consent."

That's when I started getting nervous. What did I just sign on for?

THE SOUND OF SILENCE

The next morning Judy went to Fernando's office, where I was working with him for 12 to 14 hours a day. I watched Judy go into his office and then leave without telling me much about what had transpired.

Fernando opened his office door, asked me to come in, and said simply, "Judy consents. Now we begin."

"Great," I said.

"Part one of this process: You shut up and don't say no thing to me," he said.

"Really?" I asked.

"Shh. No move lips, Joel. You listen to yourself. You're so full of noise, you can't see what the world is like around you. You can't listen to your world. So, you be shhh . . . like that."

I stopped talking.

About two days later, he gave me a little black book and said, "Fill in what you discover about being creatures of language." Then he handed me two books to read. One was Martin Heidegger's Being and Time, which was like a thousand pages of sleeping pills. The other was Humberto Maturana's book about autopoiesis and cognition in learning.

"Read those books," said Fernando. "Things change like that for you. Keep reading."

So, I would read and read, and if I could get through a paragraph without falling asleep, it was a good day. In my log I would write confused sentences, smart comments, and long, pondering questions to myself. Occasionally as we were driving around, Fernando would say, "Book, Joel." I'd hand him my log, and he'd go, "Bull (expletive)!" and throw it in the back seat.

One day, I wrote in my book: "Don't understand what Heidegger's talking about. Don't understand what Maturana is talking about."

Fernando looked at it and said, "Joel, learning happens in the body. The brain thinks. Keep reading. Your body will change."

It is like learning to ride a bicycle. You could read all the books and ask all the questions, but not until your body learned to take the proper actions did you learn to ride the bike. Once the body learned those basic actions, it could then move up the learning scale from beginner to novice, to competent, and on up to whatever level those basic actions you have integrated wanted to attain, as long as those actions continued to allow the body to learn as well.

Author of The Tipping Point and Blink, Malcolm Gladwell's states in his book Outliers that it takes 10,000 hours to be a master in a specific area.

Fernando and I went on like this for four or five months, during which time I continued to work with him day in and day out and still wasn't allowed to speak to him at all. But still I kept reading until it started to make sense, which was a strange, curious phenomenon that blew my mind.

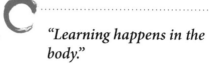

"Learning happens in the body."

One day I woke up and saw everything as language. Then, I started to write different realizations in my book. When Fernando opened it, he said, "Aha! You're awake, Joel. Part 2."

THE LISTENING OF THE LISTENING

Part 2 was what Fernando called "the listening of the listening." I was instructed to pay attention to what was going on—not in the background, but in the background of the background—that which was causing people to speak the way they spoke and to speak the concerns they spoke.

We would go to meetings with companies such as Sun Microsystems, Genentech, and others with whom he was consulting. When we walked into the room, Fernando would announce, "This is Joel. He's my boy. You don't speak to him, and he doesn't speak to you either. He just listens to your conversations in the background that are generating actions that you are unaware of. With that listening he can speculate the outcomes and actions that may take place in the future."

When we left these meetings, I would write my predictions about what would happen within these companies over the next 30, 60, and 90 days, based not on what had been said, but on what had not been spoken. It was amazing the accuracy of the predictions. I was starting to see a whole new realm of language that is invisible to us most of the time. I started to listen in on the world of Being.

When Fernando saw that I had sort of woken up, he said, "Okay. Part 3, Joel."

By then I was loving living in the silence, but now I was granted permission to speak two words. "Now 'yes and no' . . . nothing else," he said. "You accept?"

I nodded.

"Joel, yes or no? Now we move lips."

"Y-yes," I said.

That stage lasted about two weeks, and then Fernando said, "Now we begin and we build and start to understand language and the worlds we live in, Joel."

The rest is history.

THE LANGUAGE OF LIFE

From that profound understanding, we can launch into our world with the intent to make sense out of what is occurring—to think, listen, and speak generatively, to manifest our desires, and if we are fortunate enough, to have others join in our vision.

Another way of saying this is: We begin to see that the words that are coming out of our mouths not only cause outer events to be a certain way, they also cause us to be that way as well. One could say that the language we use and the words that we say invent our world,

"Most people think language lives outside of the person, that it's a "thing" that we do rather than the phenomenon that generates who we are. Our language shapes every interpretation we have and the way we speak about life. In so doing, it determines the way our world occurs in the moment."

interpretations, and ourselves in that same moment.

"Language is our connection to our world and everything connected to it. "

You could even say that at times our language speaks us. This occurs during those times when words come out of our mouths and we find ourselves saying, "Where did that come from?" And then we find ourselves taking those actions regardless.

As was said before, without language we couldn't ask people to do things for us or even offer to do things for others. Language is our connection to our world and everything connected to it. Becoming the observer of this linguistic phenomenon offers us new ways of designing our world as we speak.

Without that understanding, we are at the mercy of words—the stories we tell ourselves, the stories others tell us about ourselves. Those stories shape our decisions and our destinies, but we are not the authors of those stories. We are merely the players. Here I'm talking about authoring your life in the broadest sense . . . Being the author of our life.

QUESTIONS TO PONDER

Doing side of life:

1. *Which repetitive words would you like to change that would allow you to be more productive in your daily life? Example, I "Could" have instead of "Should" have.*

2. *In your journal, make a list of those words that you could see yourself saying and the ones you would like to use less.*

3. *Keep adding to your list as you discover new words in each area and continue to be aware of what is shifting around in your daily life. Take time to log those shifts. Writing them down seems to make them more meaningful and lasting.*

Being side of life:

1. *How do you see your life beginning to shift when using these new words, using a "Being" approach to your day, as opposed to a "Doing" approach?*

2. *If you could see yourself "Being" more present to "Being" who you are, rather than what you are doing, what would your day look like to you and those around you?*

3. *What new ways of "Being" do you see are starting to reveal themselves, ones that were not visible before, and what new actions can you see yourself now taking?*

CHAPTER 4:
THE LANGUAGE OF YOUR LIFE

"Words form the thread on which we string our experiences."

ALDOUS HUXLEY

As I've shared in the previous chapters, much of my childhood revealed to me how language limits and/or expands one's vision. This was profoundly true in the case of my father and his relationship with flying.

My dad, Joe Kimmel, was a handsome, patriotic U.S. citizen who had an unfolding passion for flying. As World War II raged in Europe, he volunteered to serve in the Royal Canadian Air Force before the U.S. had joined the war. He spent many challenging long hours up north, training Canadian pilots to fly and serve courageously overseas. During this time, he met the love of his life, Evelyn Mansell Walton, at an officer's tea social in Toronto.

They eventually moved from Canada to the U.S.A. and lived on isolated air bases in both countries—first in snow-swept Manitoba, then in hot-and-steaming Enid, Oklahoma—and Evelyn gave birth to three sons. When my dad, Joe, was honorably discharged, he decided to continue with aviation and set up his own airline, taking advantage of the airplane surplus created by the end of the war. Kansas City Southern Airways had 20 DC-3s, which hauled cargo and provided transport services connecting the fully established rail network that linked the south with cities further afield.

I have vivid memories of Dad flying my brothers and me around in his DC-3s, our mouths wide open, tears running down our cheeks because the cockpit noise was so loud, but we loved being there and flying with him.

I believe those were the happiest days of my dad's life. Unfortunately, he eventually lost the airline due to new federal antitrust regulations involving corporate conglomerates linking aviation with rail transport. Giving up the airline was tragic for him. He always loved and saw himself as being a pilot in the world, and his dream had been taken away.

When my older brother, Ed, and I were in high school, we bought a small single-engine airplane and immediately got our pilot's licenses. Our Taylorcraft taildragger was a dream come true. We took full advantage of the local Ohio cornfields and mowed our friends' meadows for the opportunity to dip and dive. I never experienced such freedom.

In Vietnam I was a helicopter crew chief. My younger brother was in the Air Force, working with B-52s. My nephew is now a pilot for Delta, and my daughter Emily works in management for a major airline.

My point is that the stories we had about my dad and his beloved airline shaped all of our lives. He never said we should be pilots or go into aviation. None of us declared those intentions publicly, and yet we ended up expressing his passion anyway.

The stories we hold and tell become the fabric of our lives.

Sometimes in living we unconsciously get carried along by a story someone else has told us, and all of a sudden it fits into our life's puzzle in so many places.

LIMITING LANGUAGE

Dad's stories gave us wings, but the stories he told himself often left him grounded.

When I was in my early teens, my uncle opened the first Volkswagen dealership in the Southeastern U.S. and offered Dad the rights to import all the Volkswagens west of the Mississippi. But Dad said, "Why would anybody want to drive those little cars around?" He couldn't see himself running Volkswagen dealerships. The possibility was outside his thinking, so he didn't take it.

The next opportunity life offered him was presented by the two gentlemen who started Fritos® corn chips after the war. They said, "Joe, we'd love to give you the business and have you come in and take it over."

"Who would want to eat corn chips all their life?" Dad asked. So he didn't take that opportunity either.

Next he had the opportunity to buy the franchise rights for McDonald's for all of northern Ohio—for $25,000. His conclusion: "Nineteen-cent hamburgers can't last."

It's interesting how some stories we tell about ourselves provide new access to different parts of our lives, while other stories shut opportunities off because we can't see ourselves Being in a new domain and trusting things will work out. The actions needed to be successful in these three opportunities were not in Dad's knowledge base at the time, and he was not comfortable in new territory. In the future I would call my brothers and joke, "Is there anything we were missing that Dad would have said 'no' to. If so, I'll go for it!"

If you look back over your life, there are probably many stories you've told or still tell about yourself that shape the way the world exists for you. Many of the stories that have the biggest impact on how you live your life are stories that attached themselves to you without you even noticing.

IN A YOU AND ME WORLD

In a you-AND-me world, you have 100% of the possibilities to have things work rather than only 50% of the possibilities in a you-OR-me world. In a you-and-me world, a conversation might sound like "I can do this if you can do that." In a you-or-me world, it might sound like "We need to do it this way or I am not going to do it." Which one best fits for you?

My dad's choices were made based on thoughts and stories he had in essence become attached to and of which he was fairly unaware.

I often compare this human linguistic phenomenon to being a fish in water. Most of us are living in the pool of language, unaware of its contribution to our well-being and survival. When we become aware of (and receptive to) the linguistic pool we have been in since birth, we gain greater control over our lives and we see all the opportunities that have been swimming right by us.

It can be as simple as taking the word "but" out of our lives. How many times have we heard ourselves saying something like this? "I want to lose weight—but I don't want to go to the gym." Using "but" conflicts with both sides of the statement.

When you use the word "and," it allows both statements to be true at the same time—and then you have a choice to make. You can go to the gym and lose weight or you can not go to the gym and little would change with your weight. The key point here is that when you insert AND in between each statement, it gives you the choice to change your life rather than having the "but" negate the choice. Give it a try AND see what you discover.

TAKING CONTROL OF YOUR STORY

My wife also spent a small part of her life being impacted by limiting language and stories. Her father was a career officer in the Foreign Service. Judy was born in Washington, D.C., but her dad was transferred to many countries throughout the world while she was growing up. As with most military families, she and her family experienced a lot of transition to foreign destinations, new homes, schools, cultures, and environments.

Out of those experiences, Judy has a thread of stories about leaving best friends behind, peering over the side of a freighter bound from Lima, Peru, for New York City, knowing that she would never see her best buddies again. Her mom said she cried through the entire voyage north.

As Judy looks back on her life today, she realizes she has an almost visceral reaction to change and transition. Realizing this pattern for herself took years; her stories were linked and built one upon the other. Now she knows that her first automatic reaction to any major change in life is mental and physical resistance, even if the change would help her get what she wants out of life. Now that she knows this about herself, she can quickly acknowledge the pattern and move on to who she wants to Be, rather than focusing on what she doesn't want to DO.

When we can identify the stories that have shaped us into who we

THE SMALL CONVERSATIONS THAT SHAPE YOUR LIFE

Take a moment to reflect over your life, and note the conversations and stories that have impacted you. It's likely that you can track the trajectory of how you've gotten to where you are based on those conversations, with yourself and others. Often these are small discussions that didn't seem to be that important at the time, yet in retrospect have had a huge impact.

are—the ones that have gotten us to this point—then we can begin to invent new tales that will take us into the next chapter of our lives, stories that reflect the way we can see ourselves Being and thriving.

QUESTIONS TO PONDER

Doing side of life:

1. What stories in your past—big and small—do you see have had a long-term impact on your actions today? Please add these stories to your journal.

2. How do you see those stories shaping your interpretation of your present-day life?

3. How would you edit one of the stories that have closed down a possibility in the past to one that opens new possibilities in the present?

Being side of life:

1. Can you see that language permeates everything you see, hear, taste, smell, sense, and feel?

2. Take a specific story from your past that has closed down opportunities and see how you would create a new narrative for the future that would allow you to thrive.

CHAPTER 5:
THE RIFF OF LIFE

"Change rooms in your mind for a day."

HAFIZ

One day while practicing a series of note sequences on my guitar, I realized that life is like a musical "riff"—a series of unexpected notes that fall into a rhythm in a piece of music. When a band performs a song, and the guitarist improvises a "riff" that everyone seems to like, this often becomes part of how the song is performed going forward.

The "Riff of Life" is a series of unexpected conversations that have fallen into a rhythm. When you look back over your life linguistically, you may find some unexpected conversations that occurred at some point in your past that allowed you to do something differently than usual or to be someone different than you would have thought you could or should be.

We all are perpetually engaged in a linguistic conversation. Those conversations shape who we are and who we think we can be. They can either be limiting conversations—like those that kept my father from taking on new opportunities—or they can open us up to accept new possibilities the universe offers to us.

I use the term "linguistically" rather loosely, as the broadest interpretation of language. One definition we apply says that we use language to interact with each other. I see language as "anything that

READY TO CHANGE YOUR TUNE? OR HOW THE RIFF CAME TO BE.

When people come to me to go through the process I created, called "The Riff," I don't try to solve their problems, change who they are, or make them into different people. Instead I engage them in new conversations (or Riffs) and help them explore a model of how we live in language.

The Riff process is designed to help you become the observer of your language. It focuses on how we speak and interact with each other, and how, in that speaking, there emerges an ability to disrupt a moment of awareness—triggering a new and different direction.

In this way you can begin to see new ways to engage in your world, ways that are natural to who you are and that will allow you to be who you can see yourself Being.

disturbs our steady state of awareness when we're in our daily life."

If somebody clapped, that could be a type of language, because it would disrupt my awareness while I was doing something else. By surprising me and interrupting what I was doing, that disruption might start me off on another thought process or inspire a new "riff."

In this chapter, I'm going to take you through the first phase of "The Riff." The focus of this process is to discover how you got to this moment . . . not psychologically but linguistically.

During this process, I invite you to participate fully. Don't read this like a lecture; instead engage with it, as if your life depends on it.

Let's begin this dialogue the way we would if you were a private client sitting in my office in Mill Valley, California.

To begin I ask you to sit down in a comfortable lounge chair. You are facing me, and there is a whiteboard behind my left shoulder.

I start by asking some questions to begin our conversation. They're simplistic questions like "Who is buried in Grant's tomb?" or "What color was George Washington's white horse?"

You know the answers, right?

Grant is buried in Grant's tomb, and Washington's white horse was obviously white. Your mind says, "Okay, that was easy."

Next I ask: "Before you were conceived, what was there for you . . . for this little physical body? What was there for you before you were born?"

Most people respond: "Nothing, black, void . . . I see black."

"Perfect," I say. "See how easy this is? I'm going to put your comment up there on the whiteboard as 'nothing.'" Then, I proceed to draw a simple black square in the middle of the whiteboard that represents nothingness.

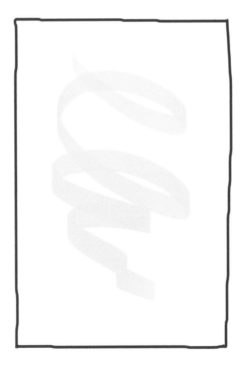

Occasionally, people respond to my first question by sharing spiritual thoughts, religious insights, or beliefs about former lives. And I say, "Okay, that's fine. Those are, however, constructs of your current mind, your imagination. REALLY though, for this physical body, you can't prove there was anything there prior to when you were conceived."

Then we move on. I say, "Now you spend nine months riding around in this amazing vehicle—your mother's womb—being well nourished in a nice, warm environment with maybe a little music filtering in and maybe a little Mexican food. All along, you're growing and being, not having intellectual experiences. Then, after sort of a brutal launch into life through a relatively short passageway, you arrive here. Then, what was there for you?"

The usual response is something along the lines of "I'm now my physical being?"

"Yeah, you're now in this body. You've come out. You've been born. You are conscious."

You reply, "There's flesh and bone and fluids."

"All of that is true, and what else is there?" I ask. "So prior there was nothing? You came from nothing, a void?"

You add, "Right. Oh, now there's something I am consciously experiencing. What I am consciously experiencing is everything so far in my universe."

I tell you that you're right. It's wild how we are born. You come out and they wrap you in this little thin blanket and go, "Isn't he/she the cutest little thing ever?" You may be experiencing the cold, noise, or bright lights of a hospital, or, if you were birthed at home, a soft environment with low lights, and maybe even a bit of music.

Everyone's arrival is different. But one of the first things we become aware of is our basic functional needs. Perhaps you want to go back from where you just came, because it's the only place you know—not just physically but consciously.

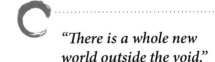

"There is a whole new world outside the void."

And over time, that changes. We become conscious of more than just our physical environment. We eventually become aware of our own thoughts—our inner voice.

ENTER THE INNER VOICE

At that point, there is something you are experiencing that is beyond pure reflex response.

When that separation initiates, an inner dialogue begins. This perception is a powerful linguistic distinction; yet, many people live for years without experiencing their inner dialogue.

If you aren't sure what I am talking about, take a moment and stop reading. Quiet your body and listen. Do you observe anything internally? Do you hear yourself talking to yourself, wondering what's next? That's the inner dialogue to which I'm referring—there are many names for it: the conscience, the ego, your talk radio, etc.

You could say early on it isn't really a dialogue, since you don't have a formal language at birth. And there is an awareness of a separation between you and the world. You begin to develop a construct that acts and reacts based upon your awareness and experiential input. As time passes, that construct becomes increasingly sophisticated, gaining more and more linguistic complexity and thus control over your actions and thoughts.

So a bit more about your arrival experience. After spending nine months in the womb, we may find ourselves wrapped in this thin blanket lying on a cold stainless steel table with bright lights all around. Where do we find our awareness going? We are becoming aware of this different environment that surrounds us.

When you find yourself having the experience of freezing, that little voice—your inner awareness—reacts: "Cry." A little while later you experience physical pains in your stomach, and you cry again. This internal phenomenon, or little voice, realizes: "I'm hungry, and the outside world puts something in my mouth." This process goes on and on, building on itself.

We start with nothing from the void and we evolve with lots of new input and reactions. We discover a limited type of communication early on. It's not words at this stage but our reactions that affect the outside world. And there's an internal phenomenon that directs our understanding of what we're seeing and experiencing out there.

So, if we go back to our birth, this world is pretty good to us right now, because everything this inner voice is urging us to do has worked and, to a large degree, saved our life. Therefore it can be depended upon to save our lives, relieving any upset. Right from the beginning this "inner voice" is our best friend, and we can trust it because discomfort has gone away.

We're getting what we need from the outside world.

One day, however, we experience a new development. This time, we're thrown a curveball. The inner voice initiates a behavior. You take an action—such as crying—but your needs don't get met.

This doesn't allow our relationship with our internal voice over time to spawn much confidence or trust and often leads to confusion. We don't know if this inner voice is telling us the truth until after the fact. So the one thing we had trusted in the beginning now leaves us not knowing if we should trust it or not.

Life, right from the beginning, is centered around this relationship between your internal voice and your external world. Thus, you exist not knowing for sure if your inner voice can be counted on to tell you the truth until you see the outcome of following it. All of this would be fine if we were not still listening to that voice as though it were the answer to all our decisions. More about this later.

What do we spend our lives seeking? Certainty, survival . . . right? This inner voice and experience is our human system that was supposed to give us assurance all the time. We quickly learn that in life, nothing is certain.

Your inner voice is part of the package and will be there for the rest of your life. The question is, how do you manage it in a way that allows you to live at peace?

The inner voice came with our package, and it has no specific plans to sabotage us. It is just trying to figure out what just happened and what might happen in the future. Either way, it is our speculation and hope that drives the information we collect and the internal conversations we have.

SHIFTING YOUR INTERNAL CONVERSATION

This inner voice follows us throughout our lives and never really goes away. In fact it's like "Talk Radio," because it is on all hours of the day and acts as if it knows everything. Many people think that in order to be happy, they need to have the little voice disappear.

You may learn and realize the Little Inner Voice will always be with us, adding its opinions and points of view, even when not called upon. The goal isn't to get it to stop, but rather to allow the voice to babble on while you stay focused on completing the task at hand. Once you realize that you are not that little voice, but rather the listener to that voice, there is a shift in your ability to be productive and content in life.

The opportunity is to find a way where you can live with it—a way that doesn't make it wrong for what it is telling you, but rather finds a way to thank it for keeping an eye out for you. After all, that Little Inner Voice is doing its best to help you survive and protect you so you don't get hurt.

I have a personal practice where, when my Little Inner Voice starts getting too loud, I thank it for watching out for me and promise I will make sure things on this side of the line go well. Since I started doing this, my inner voice has calmed down and become quieter. Try it out and see what happens. If your voice quiets down, make sure you thank it for doing so.

When we are not wrestling with our internal voice, we have the opportunity to see new possibilities that were previously hidden from view."

So here we are. In walking through this first part of The Riff, you have discovered your origins in the Void and stepped through the portal to develop an increasingly expanding and evolving inner conversation, exploring an inner voice that leads you forward in the present, impacting your choices, your thoughts, even your physical actions and reactions.

QUESTIONS TO PONDER

Doing side of life:

1. Have you identified your Inner Voice?

2. Write down any recurring stories that you find to be defining you.

3. What are the themes of these internal recurring stories, and what are they focused on?

4. Write down at least three new ways you could see yourself interacting with the stories without letting them have the same impact on you.

Being side of life:

1. What ways do you see new internal conversations shaping your days or the projects you are working on in daily life?

2. If you could shift these conversations to be more supportive for you, what would they sound like and what new ways of Being do you see them opening up and giving you?

CHAPTER 6:
THE ROLE OF THE BODY

"Our body is precious. It is our vehicle for awakening. Treat it with care."

BUDDHA

The role the body plays in language probably has more impact on how we live in our world than any other part of our linguistic conversations and interactions. Somatic teachers suggest that the body lives in the present; when paid attention to it is a source of wisdom and can generate actions.

For example, say we're walking together on some fall day in Central Park and I urgently yell, "Duck!" Your body crouches down quickly and dramatically to avoid being hit. If I say in a normal voice, "Duck," you may simply look around and reply, "I don't see any ducks around here." If we are at the end of a long drive in anticipation of a home-cooked meal and I say, "Roasted duck with mashed potatoes?" you may smile or not, depending on your culinary tastes. But if I say, "Vinegar," your mouth puckers. If I say, "I love you," your body relaxes, and if I say, "I hate you," your body responds quite differently.

The point is this: Your body is always responding to every word that is spoken or is imagined to be spoken, mostly without you thinking.

AUTOMATICITY: FASTER THAN THE SPEED OF WORDS

There's a fair amount of research that suggests that the body knows what's going to happen one or two seconds before it happens. I call this unconscious response in the body our "Automaticity."

"The body, when paid attention to, is a source of wisdom and can generate positive actions."

There are two types of Automaticity. One is Learned Automaticity, which is developed through repetitive practice—such as riding a bicycle, driving a car, or writing our name. This is one way we train our body to support us in our everyday life. The more automatic these body actions become, the more productive life seems to be.

The other type of Automaticity plays an even more influential role in our actions and how we interact with our world. It happens "before thought"—before we could even imagine anything happening at all. This type of Automaticity protects us from what the body perceives will cause us physical harm or discomfort. Sometimes this is a good thing, as it can literally save our lives. But other times, it can hinder us from taking action, simply because we fear discomfort, uncertainty, or breaking away from our own patterns.

In this chapter, we will focus on the second type of Automaticity and discover how many of our decisions have been made in response to the comfort of the body rather than out of conscious choice. Becoming aware of your own Automaticity can be powerfully liberating. The question worth exploring is: What drives your Automaticity? One place to begin observing this is in our personal habits, because habits are grounded in our body's need to feel comfortable or to be safe.

The body will do almost anything to avoid falling into discomfort or pain.

As an example, for years I loved to drink scotch. It was a manly thing. I remember seeing my dad sit in his easy chair every evening, reading the newspaper with a highball in hand. As I got older, I began having a cocktail here and there; my drink of choice was—no surprise—scotch.

"The source of our body's automaticity is the body's addiction to seeking comfort."

Over time, my Automaticity connections got more ingrained, etched into my consciousness, and increasingly entangled. I associated drinking scotch with "good times"—hanging with friends, playing guitar, smoking Camels: those were the days.

Not until I was much older did I realize the pleasure my body was experiencing while drinking scotch on the rocks was not only directly related to scotch drinking, but rather hooked to a long litany of memories, story chains, and associations—originating with my dad.

We all have our Automaticities. I have mine. You have yours. My wife has hers. Our dog has his. All biological beings have automatic actions that are ingrained in our personal and cultural matrix.

"Becoming aware of your own Automaticity can be powerfully liberating."

The interesting challenge is to become the observer of your Automaticity—not to sit in judgment of it as right or wrong, but just to notice that it is there. This gives you the chance to ensure that these habits aren't limiting your ability to be who you both want to be . . . and see yourself as being.

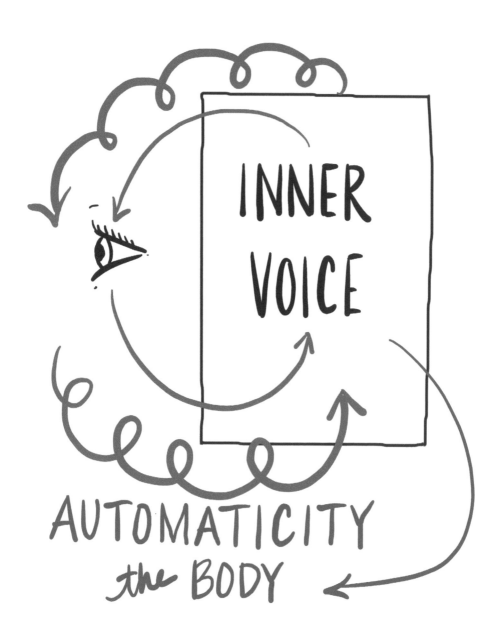

When I was volunteering for the National Park Service at the Golden Gate National Recreation Area, I was on the horse patrol. It was and still is a wonderful program. Our job was to feed the Park Service horses, clean their stalls, groom our patrol horses, and then go for a ride on some of the most beautiful trails in our country.

While I was volunteering, the rancher who lived next door gave my daughter Emily a green broke quarter horse. Green broke is a term describing a horse that has just started being trained to ride. Emily had a wonderful relationship with Edith Anne and eventually worked with her and turned her into a really excellent riding horse. As they say, however, it takes a village to raise a child, which is somewhat the same as training a horse.

Initially I started working with Edith Anne so we could trust her with Emily. One day after a rain, I started to take Edith out for a ride. I noticed that every time she came to a puddle, she would either stop or walk around the puddle. So in this case we could say that Edith had an Automaticity that kept her from walking through the puddles. Another way to say this is that her body was not comfortable around puddles, so to avoid the discomfort or fear, Edith's body took a different course. I kept working with her to ease her fear, which took what seemed to be a very long time.

One very rainy day, I decided to take Edith for a ride and see what happened. There were puddles everywhere; almost no matter where she put her hoof, it would hit a puddle. As she left the barn, she was a little resistant, but after three or four puddles in a row, she found herself walking through any water regardless of the size or depth.

The next day after the rain had stopped, I went down to the barn and rode her out on the trails, and sure enough, Edith's fear of puddles had seemed to subside; she just wandered on through any water she found in front of her. It even got to the point when we would go down to the beach, she would wander in the tideline of the surf with no worries. She had overcome the Automaticity by stepping through her fears and had overcome her fear of puddles.

AUTOMATICITY CAN LEAD TO BREAKDOWNS

Linda is a brilliant therapist with whom I sometimes collaborate. Often when she is counseling couples, she will call me in to work with the husband, while she works with the wife.

"We all have our own Automaticities; they are in our biology. The opportunity is to become aware of them and use them to our advantage."

In one such instance, Linda was coaching a couple who lived in the Berkeley Hills and felt they needed to make a move. This required selling their house in a lackluster real-estate market.

They both wanted to buy a house in St. Augustine, Florida, that was on the market for $1.6 million. Their offer was only $600,000.

The husband's intention was to get a job in the green energy field and work from home; the wife, a well-known artist, wanted to teach at a local university. And they wanted to get pregnant. Their goals amounted to an awesome and challenging list.

While my friend the psychotherapist and the wife worked in her office, I worked with the husband, Martin. We would go to the Claremont Hotel, sit on the patio overlooking the San Francisco Bay, and watch the sunset while we talked about his vision, their dreams, and who they could see themselves Being that would allow their vision to be fulfilled.

As we spent time together, I began to notice that every time I asked Martin about money, his body would react. I'd say, "So, Martin, what are you going to do about the additional money you need to buy that house in Florida?"

He would run his hands through his hair, cross his arms, and go away mentally for ten or fifteen seconds. Clearly his body and awareness shifted.

I began to discover this Automaticity and knew that when he was in his head, he wasn't really with us. His body was present, but his Being and his awareness weren't. When Automaticity kicks in, it is useful to wait until it has cycled through and take a breath, rather than trying to push through. So, I backed off and let him process.

Every six weeks, the four of us would meet in Linda's office. One afternoon, Martin and his wife were sitting next to each other on the couch, discussing what each of them had accomplished since our last meeting.

Things were moving along well until his wife said, "Honey, what are we going to do financially?"

I knew Martin's Automaticity would be kicking in. "He can't hear you," I said. "Give him a second or two."

She gave me a puzzled look.

"Just watch," I said.

Sure enough, Martin stroked his head, crossed his arms, and checked out momentarily. About five seconds later, he said, "What are we talking about?"

"Oh, my God," the wife said. "No wonder we can't talk about money! He's not there."

After we all had a good laugh, I told her, "The next time you are going to have a conversation about money, start with something like, 'Martin I would like to discuss our finances. Is now a good time?' If he says 'yes,' then carry on. If not, find another time that would work for both of you."

The punch line of this couple's story is that they moved to St. Augustine, Florida, bought the house for $600,000, and got pregnant. She got a job teaching at the university, and he got the job for an energy company working out of his home office. They now live happily (with two kids) in a home they love.

Once they started to see how most of the breakdowns they were dealing with were generated by the Automaticities triggered in their bodies—and not problems they had with each other—they were able to communicate powerfully and create the life they envisioned.

COMFORT ZONE MAGIC

There's a great family story of when our youngest daughter, Whitney, was in the process of organizing all the details for her upcoming wedding. She and Jordan had looked all over for different venues and locations for the wedding, talked to all their friends about what had worked best for them, and figured out how much the wedding would cost and how to address all the details.

The location had been chosen, the Sundance Institute and Conference Center in Utah, December 14 was the date, and the guest list had been decided. Jordan and Whitney spent hours organizing the wedding invitations and choosing the exact look that they thought would express their commitment to see that the wedding was really about the guests' enjoyment and fun rather than just Whitney and Jordan's.

Whitney made the journey up to see Judy and me to discuss the budget and how much the wedding would cost. She had done an amazing job including all the details and getting the best price possible from all the vendors. The budget was agreed upon, and we wrote Whitney a check for the amount we thought would cover the major expenditures. It was her job to stay within the budget we had agreed upon and/or to come up with any overages on their own.

Whitney flew home to start the formal invitations and addressing all the envelopes so that they were mailed out on a timely basis. Needless to say she and Jordan were very excited about the whole event and had high anticipation that all their friends would be coming to celebrate the happy occasion.

A couple weeks later I received a call from Whitney asking me about managing people's "comfort zones" so they could take new actions rather than just keep doing the old ones. The inquiry came a bit from left field.

In those days it was clear to us that Whitney grew up in the larger family conversation of how we live in language and the joy and mastery of using it to design wonderful ways of being and living in her world. She had also grown up around horses and knew the fundamentals of how to "horse whisper." She was aware that in training the horse, you "make what you want them to do easy and what you don't want them to do hard." So when she was training her horses, her real job was to manage their comfort zone. When they did something right, she would acknowledge them by using their name and stroking them for physical reinforcement.

Her horse was Lucy, a roan Appaloosa given to her by a judge who had several horses down at the barn we were using within the Golden Gate National Recreation Area. Every time Whitney would go for a ride on Lucy, she would write the judge a thank-you note and tell him where she and Lucy had gone.

One day, she received a letter from the judge on his legal letterhead saying, "Why don't you take Lucy for as long as you want and then when you're done riding her, let me know and I will take her back up to the ranch and turn her out."

Whitney rode Lucy for a long time and also started giving riding lessons to younger kids in our neighborhood. She would also teach them the secret about horse whispering.

So when Whitney called and asked about the "comfort zone," I told her it had a lot to do with the same things she learned about horse whispering. I asked what was going on that had enticed her to know more about managing people's comfort zones.

She said that she and Jordan had finished filling out and addressing all the invitations to the wedding on Sunday and had them all set up to go to the post office on Monday morning. Whitney and Jordan went off to work, and when Whitney came home, the invitations sat in the same place they had been left on Sunday night. She asked Jordan why he hadn't mailed the invitations, and he said, "I was just busy this morning and forgot. I will mail them tomorrow morning."

Whitney replied by stressing the timely nature of the task. If people didn't get the invitations early enough, they wouldn't be able to join the celebration. Jordan agreed.

Whitney arrived home on Tuesday afternoon, and there the invitations sat on the table right where they were on Sunday night. She was calling me to explore how to get Jordan on a new track. She'd had the thought that her horse whispering approach might work. I said, "Oh, perfect. It is all about reinforcing Jordan's comfort zone."

When reviewing the situation, we observed that Whitney had started with a clear request of Jordan, and both she and he had agreed on a time and date for when the invitations would be mailed. That's a great start. Many times, what causes problems is when each person assumes that the other knows exactly what they want, when in fact each of them has their own interpretation of what they need. Occasionally their actions are not in sync, and they find themselves having to start over again.

In agreements, make sure everyone knows exactly what the outcome will look like and what the intended outcome actually is before anyone takes any actions.

Another powerful tool that works is acknowledgment. One of the things our physical body loves to hear is its name used when it is acknowledged for something. Here is a simple test. If I say, "Good job," what you might hear is your body asking you, "Who is he talking to?"

Try this out. Pick something that you would like to be acknowledged for and just say "Good job" for doing X. Chances are your body is now asking yourself who you are talking to. Now if I say to you, "Good job_____ (fill in your name)," you can feel your body receive the acknowledgment because your comfort zone seems to fall into place. As we said before, the body is addicted to seeking comfort, and once it finds it, it will repeat the patterns to stay in that comfort zone.

So here's the punch line I gave to Whitney: "When Jordan comes home this evening, find something you can acknowledge him for using his name. So if Jordan did something that was meaningful to you in alignment with how you would like to have a specific task accomplished, say 'Thank you, Jordan. I appreciate it.'"

So Jordan got home that evening, and she didn't say anything about the invitations. At some point, Whitney found herself authentically acknowledging him for something that truly meant something to her, using his name.

The next morning Jordan left for work before Whitney did, and as Whitney was leaving the house, she noticed that the invitation box was gone. That evening when Jordan came home, Whitney said, "Thanks, Jordan, for mailing the invitations. That was great."

"Acknowledging the body by name and deed is really the icing on the cake."

They had a great dinner that night, talked in detail about what needed to be done for the wedding, and went to bed with smiles on their faces. Whitney said, "Thanks, Jordan, for such a wonderful evening," and "I love you very much."

The next morning, Whitney left early for work. When she came home that evening, Jordan was there and the house had been cleaned, there were fresh flowers on the dining room table, and Jordan was cooking dinner for the two of them. Guess what Whitney said to Jordan?

We received another call from Whitney the next day. She was excited and alive about how amazing it is when you acknowledge people, not only by addressing them by name, but also by acknowledging them for what you appreciate about them. It is interesting to note that Whitney's actions were all driven because that was the way she wanted their relationship to be into the future.

Automaticity is the body's language—it speaks when it needs the comfort that words can't provide. Learning to interpret Automaticity, in ourselves and others, enables us to overcome the barriers that keep us from connecting and moving forward. Acknowledging the body by name and deed is really the icing on the cake.

> *"Your beliefs become your thoughts,*
>
> *Your thoughts become your words,*
>
> *Your words become your actions,*
>
> *Your actions become your habits,*
>
> *Your habits become your values,*
>
> *Your values become your destiny."*
>
> Mahatma Gandhi

RISK AVERSION

Except in the case of mating males, the physical body of a human, or almost any species, will do its best to avoid ever putting itself at risk or discomfort unless it's to save a member of its own species.

For example, you walk into your local grocery store and spot someone you have neglected to talk to for some time. Perhaps you owe them a call because they have lost a loved one and you don't know what to say, or you are embarrassed to greet them for some other reason. Before you know it, you have walked to the baby food aisle, halfway across the store, and your youngest just started college.

The physical body will take you physically away from things it considers to be stressful. As you start to observe this phenomenon, you can begin to monitor and manage it so that you're actually choosing where you'd like to find yourself, rather than being dragged around by your body's never-ending search for comfort.

Our bodies are addicted to comfort, so when we need to make a choice between two options—one that generates comfort and peacefulness and another that generates stress or uncertainty—we tend to opt for the former. We even have sayings that reinforce these choices: "Boy, that feels great," or "I feel like I made the right decision." Unless we make decisions out of clear awareness, we'll go with what feels right, rather than what we know is right.

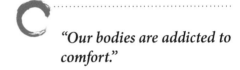

"Our bodies are addicted to comfort."

MANAGING THE COMFORT ZONE

The body wants to spend its time in the comfort zone. That's its job—to keep you safe and at peace with the world around you. But your brain knows better. The comfort zone feels good, but it's not always the place where change or growth happens. Most often, becoming who you see yourself "Being" requires you to take action into new and unexplored territory—and that could be the discomfort zone!

If you look back at problems or conflicts in your life, you may notice that some of the choices you made to "feel good" were often what generated those problems in the first place.

This moment is much like the old adage of "keeping up with the Joneses." You see that your neighbors have purchased something new that you should get because they look like they are having so much fun with it. You begin to work a little harder because the cost of that product is just "a little" outside your budget. You continue to do the extra work, and along the way, you may even question whether you really need the widget. Well the day comes when you make the big widget purchase, and you open up the package and start to use it. That night buyer's remorse sets in, as well as the conversation about "Why did we do this in the first place?"

What looked like something you needed to be happier shortly becomes something that may rob you of some of the happiness you had before.

So the next time you find yourself thinking that something will make you happier because a good friend has purchased one, take a breath and check in with your bigger Self. See that true joy may actually come from knowing that you have the willingness to make the tough decisions. Those decisions allow you to be true to yourself rather than keeping up with those that surround you.

Powerful people are those willing to intentionally take their bodies into the discomfort zone, because they know that stepping through to the other side may unlock unlimited possibilities and offer a bigger space for them to "Be" themselves.

This doesn't always mean you need to spend all your time making the tough choices or doing what feels uncomfortable. It doesn't mean spending your time in your personal comfort zone isn't needed. Instead, it means becoming aware of the Automaticity that may be keeping you in your comfort zone. Then take a breath and see what actions you can take. And from this new perspective, take the actions that will continue to allow you to move forward in your world, choosing from a new place that is allowing you to be.

Recently I was introduced to Charlie, a very intelligent young cybersecurity specialist who wanted to address his fear of speaking in groups and sharing his new ideas. He was a handsome young man and very well spoken, yet shy.

His story was that every time he walked into a room, he found himself being nervous and wanting to hide. He also knew, however, that what he had to offer was valuable and would make a difference to his group and others in the room. When I asked him what was holding him back, he said he didn't know, but he always seemed to be stuck there.

We started to talk about the body's comfort zone and how it would take us away from things it felt were dangerous for us and would cause us discomfort. The more we talked,

"Powerful people are those willing to intentionally take their bodies into the discomfort zone, because they know that stepping through to the other side may unlock unlimited possibilities."

the more Charlie started to see that there was little to be afraid of. No one was going to hurt him; they weren't going to throw anything at him. So what was the fear?

As he sat there, he began to smile. When I asked him what he was smiling about, he said, "At myself."

I asked, "What about yourself?"

He said, "It is all the stories I have made up about what might happen, rather than what could happen if I spoke."

When I asked him what happens to people around him when he does speak and share his ideas, his face brightened up. He then shared a variety of great stories of successful moments in his life. They were there; he had just buried them.

I asked him about what new actions he could see himself taking in the future that would allow him to be more self-expressive. He realized that all he needed to do was to step through the discomfort, and from that side of the line, then share his insights.

He then asked what he could do that would give him a better chance of feeling confident even when his imagined fear was present.

I responded, "The one thing to do anytime you feel nervous or afraid is to take a deep breath, in and out, and then see what your world looks like. Breathing like this to regroup is a standard practice for athletes, performers, and even for you just before you take a big step into the unknown. What does your body do just before you jump into a swimming pool? It takes a big breath. So the next time you find yourself getting nervous or worried about what is coming next or what to do now, breathe."

Another recommendation I gave Charlie was to thank his "Little Voice" for keeping an eye out for him, and while it was doing that, to let it know that he was going to continue to stay focused on giving a great speech.

"So the next time you find yourself getting nervous or worried about what is coming next or what to do now, breathe."

Charlie continued to come back to give me updates on his progress. He has found himself being more willing to speak in front of groups and discovered that the more he was willing to step away from his comfort zone to a discomfort zone, the more the audiences enjoyed his speech.

I still receive occasional phone calls from Charlie with updates, and the last time we spoke, asked what he was doing at the present. He said his job was leading public presentations at cybersecurity conferences all over the country. When I asked him what he had learned over the years, he said, "Don't be afraid of stepping through the discomfort zone, because greatness lives on the other side."

"Security is mostly a superstition. It does not exist in nature, nor do the children of men as a whole experience it. Avoiding danger is no safer in the long run than outright exposure. Life is either a daring adventure, or nothing."

Helen Keller

GORDON'S STORY: STEPPING THROUGH THE COMFORT ZONE

A new client came to me in the midst of trying to discover or figure out what his next step should be in his career. He was a very successful pharmaceutical salesman, tops in his company and field, but at the same time, he wasn't feeling fulfilled by the work he was doing.

He started our conversation with that familiar statement, "I just don't know what to do at this time in my career." As we continued to talk, he shared his idea of taking time off and going back to grad school to get his Business MBA. He had read that would be a good possibility for him to investigate. Gordon wanted to address some of the pertinent concerns that he had around making that transition and moving away from the financial comfort he was living in at the time. At the end of our meeting, he said he would do the research and would then love to come back and have a discussion about the actions he should take.

At our next meeting, he reported that since we'd last met, an interesting thing had happened. While he was researching grad school, he'd received a couple of different offers from other companies, one being a start-up in the process of bringing into existence three new products. He said he was very excited about that possibility because the person who had spoken to him about this had

had a very successful career of taking start-ups and eventually selling them for a significant profit.

As we continued, Gordon did say that he was still dealing with the discomfort and uncertainty of stepping away from his sales position to enter an unknown journey. When I asked what was driving his decision, he said his commitment to being a great father and husband and having a wonderful family came first. Inside of that was included his responsibility to have financial resources to allow that to happen. He did say that he was fortunate to have the financial backing to be able to take advantage of either of those opportunities.

I asked him which of those two opportunities would allow him to keep his promise to his wife, the family, and himself. He said he thought he would stay focused on the start-up possibility, give it his best shot, and reassess things in six months.

I bumped into Gordon about six months later, and he said he was about to become the father of twins and was also looking into the possibility of relocating and accepting a new position at a new company. When I asked him if he was concerned about all the change and uncertainly, he looked me straight in the eye and said, "No. I have the trust in myself and the ability to have the right conversations that will keep me and my family thriving." He continued by saying that from our conversations, he discovered that it is much easier to step through the discomfort than it is to sit around worrying about what might not happen.

COMFORT ZONES UNITE

Often our comfort zones lure us into missing opportunities—to grow, change, take on new opportunities, and make new connections. But this isn't always the case. Comfort, after all, can be a good thing, especially in certain areas of our lives, like relationships.

In fact, sometimes our comfort zones attract us to other people. Say you go to a party and see someone across the room. Your eyes meet, and you can feel your comfort zone fall into place. You think, Oh, good. I'd love to meet that person, but I don't want to walk over and just introduce myself because that would feel awkward.

If that person's comfort zone has connected with yours before the evening is over, your physical bodies will invariably bump into each other, and your little voice will say, Oh, my gosh. Isn't this interesting? We should talk.

When you start to become aware of your comfort zone, and you find yourself mutually attracted to each other's comfort zones, your conversations change. Your bodies are already present with each other, so your connection could go deeper, and faster. In fact, this often is the beginning of a marriage and/or lasting love.

I met my wife, Judy, on a blind date. I had plans to meet my close friend Mike, whom I hadn't seen for about nine months. It was the day before Memorial Day, and Mike was dating a girl named Dottie, who attended a small liberal arts college in northern Ohio. He called Dottie and asked if she could find a date for his long-time buddy Joel.

The next day, I drove to Nemeth's Bar and Grill in a small Ohio town. I arrived an hour late—my usual pattern in those days—and walked in to find a typical college town bar. It was dark and smoky, with a neon sign flashing "Rolling Rock Beer" in the window. I found Mike at a booth with two attractive girls. I slid in across from Mike and immediately began talking to him.

We had a lot to catch up on and rushed into a conversation about how much we missed our beloved summer cottages in Canada, water skiing on the lake, how Mike was doing at Kenyon as a senior, how my mom was managing after my dad's untimely death, and so on. Mike asked me questions about our airplane, what my plans were, and what to do about the draft and Vietnam.

Truthfully, we mostly ignored the girls for a while. Then, finally, we got the last call for drinks from the bartender, and I turned and looked at Judy. She was beautiful, and not just physically. There was something more; it landed in my heart. We were clearly attracted to each other, and I remember thinking, You know, Joel, if you marry this woman, you will have a brilliant life.

It was at that moment that my comfort zone connected with Judy's comfort zone. Since that evening at the local bar, like all couples, we have gone through a lot of ups and downs. I got drafted and went to Vietnam while she protested the war at Kent State. We both had very challenging times and intense decisions to make during that phase of our relationship, and we experienced some fairly serious actions and personal reactions. What held us together, then and now, is a quality Judy and I have had together, even after forty-eight years of marriage—the ability to allow the other person's comfort zone to recover by being around the other.

It doesn't so much live in what we say; it lives in who we can allow ourselves to Be for the other. We've had our relationship challenges, but we've allowed our comfort zones to be available to each other in a way that allows us to move forward in our lives. The same is true for our two daughters. They are both powerful women—both personally and professionally—and one thing they profoundly understand is they can always call home, get back in touch with their comfort zones, know what it is to be cared for, and from there go back out into the world.

USE THE LAW OF ATTRACTION, THE POWER OF RESONANCE

Someone asked me the other day as I was commenting on children's personal spaces about the whole attraction issue. How individuals, both children and adults, either attract people or repel them based upon how they feel at the time. My friend was questioning how that dynamic relates to something that a lot of people talk about called The Law of Attraction, a book from Abraham-Hicks Publications.

HORSE LESSONS, THE LAW OF ATTRACTION

One of the arts I was fortunate enough to learn was the art of shoeing horses. It's quite an extraordinary art, to be that connected to something so large and at the same time so fragile with their comfort zones.

As we said above, we all have our Automaticity; you've got yours, I've got mine, our dog has hers, our cat has his, and our friends have theirs as well. It seems to me all biological entities are driven by their addiction to seeking comfort and avoiding being harmed.

Back to when I was volunteering for the horse patrol at the Golden Gate National Recreation Area, I would work with kids who had come from the inner city. They would arrive running around; just to be out in the open spaces of the park was a gift for each one of them. Once things calmed down, I'd invite them over to meet one of the patrol horses. The goal was for them to learn how to meet a horse in a way that the horse was glad to be with them.

I would use our quarter horse, Edith Anne, to work with the children. The kids would be all grouped up around the corral and very close to her. She had a halter on, and with her lead rope just falling to the ground, Edith could move any way she wanted to. I would ask for a volunteer who wasn't having fun or was afraid to come out and pick Edith's lead rope up and bring her over to me.

A hesitant boy came out of the group and started to walk toward Edith, and she moved away from him. When I asked him to stop, Edith would stop too.

I'd then pick someone who was excited and having fun to go pick up the lead rope and bring Edith to me. As this young girl started to walk out of the group, Edith's head came up. Edith started to move toward the girl, and they met sort of halfway in between. Edith stopped moving, and the girl took the rope and led Edith Anne over to me.

The kids thought it was some kind of magic, but as the morning went on, the boys and girls started to see that who they were being around Edith encouraged her to either come toward them or move away. Eventually one of the kids looked at me and said, "This is like meeting grown-ups too, isn't it?" The kids then started to ask questions about why this happened and how it works with people.

The punch line was that we all have our comfort zones, and our physical bodies have the ability to sense one another's comfort zones. If you are in a happy comfort zone for yourself, chances are people around you will be happy. If you're in a grumpy or less positive comfort zone, there's a good chance that everyone around you will be grumpy. It's as if the world around us is a perfect indicator of who we are being for others in that moment.

Toward the end of the morning, I got a bucket of old horseshoes out and all the kids cheered. When I asked them what they were cheering about, they said horseshoes are good luck, and if you can make a wish on a horseshoe, it might come true. I responded, "Well that certainly is possible, and Edith Anne wants for each of you to have one of her old horseshoes to make a wish."

Hands flew up, each child wanting to be the first to make a wish and get the horse-shoe. I handed one to one of the youngest kids in the group, they were all in fourth and fifth grade, and I asked, "What is your wish?"

The young Hispanic boy looked me straight in the eye and said, "I wish my mom and dad would stop arguing so our friends would come back over to her house and visit more." He took the horseshoe with one of the biggest grins I've ever seen on a child's face in my life.

Next was a girl who came forward and said, "I want to be a mentor for other girls in my neighborhood so that they know that they can be proud of being a girl. I want them to know that they're smart and can learn anything."

I presented her with an old rusty horseshoe. She held it with both hands and walked back to the group of kids, some patting her on the back as she joined in with them. This went on until all the kids had come forward and made their wish.

As I looked over the kids, each holding their own horseshoe, I saw their teachers were moved to tears. At that moment I held up another horseshoe and began asking the teachers for their wishes, giving each a horseshoe. When the teachers spoke their wishes, the kids listened in silence. After the last horseshoe was given, they all cheered and held their horseshoes up in unison with the teachers.

"When we become the observer of our comfort zones, both positively and negatively, we are always in the doorway of the next word spoken or the next thought taken to transform future moments for both our Self and those around us."

That was such a wonderful morning, observing kids discovering that they already know how they can live in the world; it's quite moving. The last tip that Edith and I gave the girls and boys was that they needed to make sure they held the horseshoe so the opening was pointing up, because that made sure the magic wish would stay alive in the shoe.

At the end of the packed morning full of nature, adventure, fun, and games, the boys and girls held their horseshoes up with huge smiles on their faces and waved as they walked away. They had experienced both the law of "horse attraction" and a bit of magic on the side.

Edith spent the rest of her productive days patrolling and passed away one Valentine's Day, which seemed appropriate for such an amazing horse who loved to be with people young and old in the great outdoors and who overcame her fear of puddles.

When we become the observer of our comfort zones, both positively and negatively, we are always in the doorway of the next word spoken or the next thought taken to transform future moments for both our Self and those around us.

Once again life is a gift to be enjoyed, not struggled with. The magic all lives in who we're Being about what we're Doing in each moment.

THE PUNCH LINE

The punch line, I think, in The Law of Attraction is that "likes" attract each other. So if you look at your life, when you're in a good mood, you've noticed everybody around you is in a good mood. If someone comes up to you who is not in a good mood, you find your physical body moving away from them . . . unconsciously most of the time. You may wonder why you're standing so far away, or wanting to walk away. It's because your body is not comfortable and doesn't experience its comfort zone with the other person for some reason.

Our feelings and actions could be because of a story we made up about why the person is the way they are, or some other phenomena that is invisible to us at the time. This may all boil down to a sense of resonance. Energy that is spiraling down takes other energy with it. Energy that is spiraling up moves it in the opposite direction, upward.

The point is, if you start to observe your Automaticity and how people are moving around you, you can get a real sense of the mood your body is in during a social situation. Horse whispering and people whispering are pretty much the same thing.

"Energy that is spiraling down takes other energy with it. Energy that is spiraling up moves it in the opposite direction, upward."

When I'm working with people, I make sure that I am in my comfort zone, or, as lots of people call it, being centered, being present, in place. I know that if my body's centered or in its comfort zone, the other person's body (and I'm really talking about physical bodies, not intellects, minds, or brains) will come close to meeting mine and experience being in a safe environment. That experience opens up possibilities for conversations that people couldn't imagine and grows their ability to make contributions to many.

The real opportunity here is to start to become the observer of the Automaticity of your body and to manage your comfort zone. If you can keep returning yourself to your comfort zone or to being centered, you win. When you become aware of your Automaticity and that of the people around, that awareness gives you a new way to move. If you're upset or frustrated about something in a person, their body senses that and it just makes the conversation or interaction very difficult.

WHEN COMFORT ZONES COME APART

While our comfort zones can help us connect with others, conflict with loved ones can also disrupt our comfort zones.

Perhaps there's a comment or conversation that takes place with your spouse out of your comfort zones, and your bodies start growing apart. Every time that one subject comes up, the comfort zones between you move farther away from one another. If not checked, the eventual outcome is often separation or even divorce.

What do you do if you find yourself in a similar situation? I suggest looking back over the conversations that initiated the discomfort and inviting the other person to do the same. Then you can do your best to rebuild the comfort zone and, in turn, your relationship.

"It's not about being right or whose fault it was, but about trying to understand the other's interpretation, what they were concerned about, and where your story wasn't providing comfort."

Many times resolution may start with an apology for what happened and the conversation that was the source of the problem, followed by having a meaningful conversation about how to recover your respective comfort zones. It's not about being right or whose fault it was, but rather about trying to understand the other's interpretation, what they were concerned about, and where your story wasn't providing comfort.

Judy and I have had these moments, but we have always had the conversations we needed to have to reunite our comfort zones. Sometimes the healing took place in the moment of speaking; other times it would require us revisiting the conversation until we both could see the right path to take.

My client Janis was in a relationship that was wonderful, energized, and fun. Then it fell apart.

When she spoke to me about it, they'd already broken up. After hearing about the comfort zone phenomenon, she realized that when they'd met, their comfort zones had fallen into alignment and stayed close to each other for quite a while. Then one of them said something caustic that disrupted their comfort zones.

All of a sudden, their bodies didn't have a safe zone where they could be comfortable around each other. One thing led to another, and they slowly stopped going out as often or getting intimate because their comfort zones had lost the physical attachment for each other. Rather than going back and addressing the moment where their comfort zones began to diverge, they just kept moving apart. They never slowed down enough to notice until too much damage had been done.

Longevity in relationships happens when people maintain conversations that allow the comfort zones of their physical bodies to coexist. You need to be awake enough to experience the loss and lack of comfort—in other words, to notice the problem before it's too late. When you do this, you have the awareness of choice and the opportunity to recover the connection between your comfort zones.

I am sure we have all experienced a bump in the road in a specific area of a relationship and then decided to let it go—to carry on as if it hadn't happened or didn't mean anything. Ignoring it for a while seems to work, but then that specific situation shows up in another conversation. This time the conversation seems much more intense and uncomfortable. When you think about letting it go, it just becomes more intense and your body becomes more rigid and less willing to work things out. Our basic "fight or flight" mechanism goes into overdrive, and the situation begins to look hopeless.

"Longevity in relationships happens when people maintain conversations that allow the comfort zones of their physical bodies to coexist."

Now here we must make a choice—to revisit the moment and start the conversation in a more peaceful and collaborative way, and potentially repair the lost connection between the comfort zones, or to let our bodies' need for comfort drive us further apart.

Becoming the observer of your Automaticity, and learning to manage your comfort zone around people, is a huge opportunity to live in a way where you have more meaningful conversations, and deeper connections, with the people around you.

It is your willingness to see the bigger contribution, rather than being right just one more time, that propels this closeness of the comfort zones. How about being compassionate and understanding? Working to seek clarity in a way that will allow all sides to be heard and honored? All of these actions can be taken for the sake of the relationship, the future, and the closeness of your comfort zones. That's a position of power. You stand a far greater chance of "Being" who you want to be when your focus is on the bigger contribution.

"It is your willingness to see the bigger contribution, rather than being right just one more time, that propels this closeness of the comfort zones."

AUTOMATICITY AND YOUR OWN BODY

Always do your best to acknowledge yourself by name when you find your body taking the actions that are in alignment with the vision you have for your "Self." Your body will repeat these actions to receive another acknowledgement.

Without the acknowledgement by name, the body will take other actions trying to figure out whether it is doing things right or wrong. Your body's identity this time around is what its name is. Mine happens to be Joel. So when I acknowledge it by name, I say, "Good job, Joel," or "Joel, thanks for taking those actions." When I see it taking those actions in the future, I say the same thing.

As we said earlier, our Automaticity is caused by the body's addiction to seeking comfort. When the body hears its name being connected to a positive experience, it will take those actions again. So

"When the body hears its name being connected to a positive experience, it will take those actions again."

when I say "Good job, Joel," I am reinforcing that my body will take those actions again.

HABITS, THEY ARE REPLACEABLE

Rather than trying to stop a bad habit, start another one that is easier. For example, when I wanted to stop drinking to get in shape for the big San Diego Crew Classic regatta, I made a promise to myself that I would be in the best shape I could be in by the time of the race, and I would follow what I thought were the best practices to get there.

When I looked at the project, I realized that drinking alcohol probably would not be the best thing to keep my fitness promise. So what I did was allow my body to do the same actions it was doing except I had it drinking ginger ale or soda water. After each drink I would say, "Good job, Joel," for drinking ginger ale, and very soon it lost the desire for the alcohol and wanted to keep drinking ginger ale, a new habit. Eventually my body's desire for alcohol had pretty much gone away.

We went to the highly anticipated regatta that year and won our races, which was a tremendous accomplishment. The San Diego Crew Classic was one of the biggest regattas in the country and drew crews from all parts of the country. After we received our coveted trophies, we all went to the beer tent. Someone handed me a beer, and as I got it up to my lips, I heard my body saying, "Joel, you'll feel better if you don't drink that." So I put it down and thought I would try it again later. Thirty minutes later, I picked it up again, and as it reached my lips, I heard the same voice saying, "Joel, don't drink that." So I put it down and did not try to pick up a bottle again that day.

It has now been years since that race, and I have continued with that new habit. Every time I bring any type of alcoholic drink to my lips, I hear that familiar voice say, "Joel, don't drink that."

The substitution of ginger ale for beer seems to have worked for my body.

Now it is not that I don't like to drink, I loved a gin and tonic in the summer and scotch in the winter. Currently, I just seem to be keeping my promise with my body. In the future I may hear my body say, "Go ahead, Joel, and drink that." I will then have the choice to drink it or not. Not because I can, but because I choose to.

So now when you want to change a behavior in life, think about just substituting that behavior for an action equally or more pleasurable.

QUESTIONS TO PONDER

Doing side of life:

1. Knowing that each of us has our own Automaticity, as everyone does, what Automaticities do you see those around you might have, and how do you see yourself responding to them?

2. Do you experience any strong repetitive actions or reactions to various situations and people in your life? Please add them to your journal.

3. How do you see yourself experiencing your comfort zone? Are you in touch with it? Who fits nicely in your comfort zone today?

Being side of life:

1. Have you begun to see how your body's addiction to seeking comfort has warned you or taken you away from what it might consider to be dangerous? An example of that might be seeing someone you don't want to talk to and then finding yourself walking another way to avoid having to talk with them.

2. Regarding the Automaticity of your body, where do you see it in your day-to-day life and what new actions do you see yourself taking? As you become aware of the Automaticity, how do you see this awareness altering your choices in the future?

CHAPTER 7:
ASSESSMENTS YOU LIVE IN

*"At the end of the day, when I surrendered and
I knew that I am not what I believed I am,
it was a big relief. It was freedom."*

DON MIGUEL RUIZ

M y working definition of Assessments is that they are the stories, points of view, and decisions we've made in the past that made sense out of that particular moment in life. More importantly, we are still using those same Assessments today to make sense out of our experiences in the present.

The difficulty is that this current moment is not the same as the first moment we used the Assessment, and therefore the effect may be somewhat sketchy—to say the least.

The choices we've made around those Assessments either open up new opportunities for us or close them down.

Look back in your life: What

"Assessments are the stories, points of view, and decisions we've made in the past that made sense out of that particular moment in life."

Assessments have you made that color your view of yourself or the world around you? I bet there is a long list:

- Only rich people get ahead.
- School isn't for everybody.
- It's bad to be weak.
- I'm too fat.
- I'm not as good, smart, talented, etc., as (fill in the blank).

The list goes on. How did you hold those Assessments then, and how do you hold them today?

In my childhood, I collected lots of Assessments—that I was a good athlete, that people liked hanging around with me, and that I wasn't smart like my big brother. Some of those assessments were useful and propelled me to thrive. I don't think I would have run the Western States 100-mile Ultra-Run if not for my Assessment that I was an athletic "winner."

On the other hand, the Assessment that I was not as smart as my brother held me back and made me feel like I couldn't perform academically, and thus hindered my education during my youth, causing me not to trust myself in class and to give up on challenging homework and tests.

One example of an unproductive Assessment might be that you feel your boss is too demanding. She has unfairly, in your opinion, passed you over for a sales bonus in the spring quarter when you were out of work for a substantial period of time due to elective surgery.

That may or may not be true. Others on your team may feel she is a good boss and has been a fair judge of everyone's performance. You may also have had a bad fall quarter bringing in advertising sales; you may feel she thinks you're too old for the job or not aggressive enough. All these Assessments lead you not to trust her or your team. Without further investigation and inquiry, you are stuck in that story. We've all made these types of decisions in our lives.

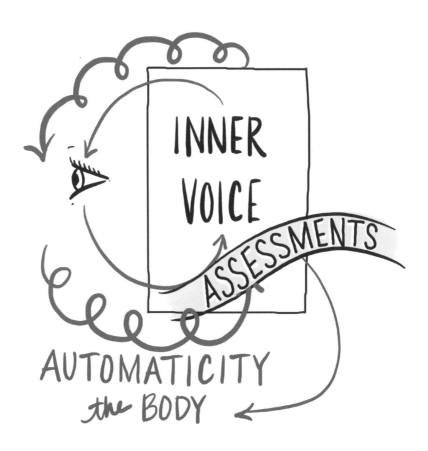

ASSESSMENT, GROUNDED OR NOT?

Here a word of caution: Assessments are not necessarily the truth. Often, we have made them in a flash and falsely act as if they are fact. One way to remind our Self that they are not the truth is to ground them—to determine whether they can be validated.

For instance, you could ask another person who was present in a situation for his or her interpretation, and then see how close it is to yours. If it is similar to yours, you could say it was a "grounded assessment," and you could use it in a future conversation to suggest new possibilities related to your current conversation.

"Assessments are not necessarily the truth. Often, we have made them up in a flash and falsely act as if they are fact."

This is an important distinction to understand, let's see how it works.

ABOUT HER DAD

It's not just our Assessments about ourselves that can cause us problems. Assessments about the people closest to us or things that happen to us in life can also weigh us down and contribute to confusion and blame.

One late fall day I met Sasha, who was referred to me by a former client. Sasha was a vibrant and excited woman and a great artist. She sat in my office and gazed out at the view, clearly concentrating on something. When I asked what she would like to talk about, she said, "My relationship with my father."

"Sounds great," I said. "Please tell me your story."

She told me about the difficulty she'd had with her father over the years, trying to understand why he was the way he was, so domineering and critical, and why he spoke to her so harshly.

We began talking about Assessments she may have had about her father—that he was rigid, old-fashioned, impatient, unforgiving—and the impact they had on her. Like layer after layer of fog, they had clouded her mind. Sasha started to see that most of the thoughts or feelings she had about her dad lived in her long-held Assessments about him, and that kept her from being able to see him with new eyes each time he spoke.

Finally, she said, "I'm amazed at how my Assessments have been keeping me from seeing my dad as he is now—an older, successful gentleman, brought up in New England, having survived the Depression and World War Two, supporting a very successful family, spending time with his grandchildren, managing family properties and private enterprises."

At the end of the session, I asked what she learned today that would allow her to live a more peaceful life and what new actions she could take as a result of that discovery. As she stood framed in the doorway, she looked over her shoulder, paused with a smile on her face, and said, "I'm going home to write my father a love letter and thank him for the life he was able to give me and my siblings."

"When we discover something new, or our interpretation of a situation changes, we then have the opportunity to redesign our view of it and thus our world."

This transformation in perspective may seem difficult to understand—how could Sasha go from having such a difficult time being with her father to wanting to thank him for the incredible, privileged life she was able to live? Her Assessments had shifted. I've always been fascinated by how we all have the power to shift our understanding. The insight can be instantaneous.

When we discover something new, or our interpretation of a situation changes, we have the opportunity to redesign our view of it and thus our world. Just by becoming aware of our Assessments in that domain, we are freed from the hidden meaning behind those Assessments, so we can take a leap of faith and move on.

Through the years I have come to the realization that we have all, without exception, been giving life our best shot. While we might be impacted by the world around us and distracted by pressing issues, I suggest that, right in that moment, we are giving it our very best.

> *"Through the years I have come to the realization that we have all, without exception, been giving life our best shot."*

If we could have done it any better, I suggest we would have. While at that moment it might not have looked like it, in retrospect, is does. Yes, we might have one of "those days," or the other person we are with might be having one, but we are both doing our very best to get through.

So if we can see that this might be true, then who gives us the permission to treat others as if it does not apply to them? We all live in different worlds, and their other worlds are different than ours. Honoring the other for the effort they are and have been giving their life can create a new, meaningful relationship. Then life can become a collaborative series of conversations to explore the other's interpretation rather than whether it is the right interpretation in your eyes.

When Sasha saw that her dad had been giving it his best shot, she also could see that right beside that was an opportunity to begin a new kind of relationship and understanding to live in.

When I saw her a few months later, she told me that she and her dad were doing great and she and her son had stepped into a whole new world as well, a world that allowed them to have meaningful conversations about their "interpretations" of the situation rather than whether he was doing life right or wrong.

THE TRACK MEET

It was my senior year at Mayfield High School, and I was representing my school at the county track meet. My mom had driven me down to Mentor, Ohio, where the events were taking place, and stayed to cheer me on. By the end of the afternoon, I had participated in—and won—several events.

My final challenge loomed ahead. I was high-jumping and had cleared six feet. It was two inches over my head, and I'd missed six-foot, two-inches twice. I had to run the third leg in the mile relay with my other teammates before I could do this third and last high jump. After the run, I was exhausted. My mom was standing at the apron of the high jump by my sweats, and I could've just knocked the bar off and said, "Let's go home." It was the last thing in the day. But I took a breath, set my sights high, gave it a shot, and missed passing the bar significantly.

As I was collecting my track gear, I thought I heard my mom say, "You know, Joel, you just never have it when the going gets tough."

I was shocked and found myself in a pickle because I loved my mom. If I had asked her if she really said what I thought she did, the comment would've killed me; if I asked her and she hadn't said it, it would've killed her. I lived with that conflict, and that Assessment, for only forty years. It could have been for the rest of my life.

So, during much of my life, every time I thought something was going to be tough, I found myself struggling with that long-ingrained Assessment: that I didn't have what it took when the going got tough. I've had a great life even with that haunting the back of my mind, but the question always loomed over my shoulder.

Forty years went by, and one day I was going to visit my mom. This was a few months before she passed on. She was back in Ohio in a lovely retirement community surrounded by lush gardens, a canopy of shade trees, and the smell of spring blossoms. I'd asked how she wanted to spend the day, and she'd said she would like to go down to the pond, sit in the glider, and talk about all the great times we'd had together in our lives.

As we glided by the pond, we reminisced over my high school antics, including ones I'd always thought she never knew about. Our conversation grew quiet, and then she said, "You know, Joel, there was that county track meet."

I sat there a moment, took a breath, felt myself shrink physically and mentally, and said, "Yeah, Mom, there was."

She looked me right in the eye. "You know, at the track meet, I wanted you to know that I was so proud of you. I wanted everybody in the stadium to know you were my son. What you did that day was so amazing."

"Thank you." Feeling a little release, I replied, "Remember when I missed six-two?"

"Yes," she said. "If you hadn't run the quarter, you might've been able to do it, but you were exhausted."

"When I was putting my sweats on and you were standing there, I swore I heard you say, 'You know, Joel, you never have it when the going gets tough.'"

"Joel Bruce Kimmel," she said, "I would have never said that to you, ever. I was so proud of you."

I couldn't believe it. That track story had been following me for decades. My experience was shocking. Finally, after all these years, I could let that Assessment go.

Once we start to discover the Assessments that have been shaping our stories, we can choose new actions and write new stories for ourselves. But most people keep responding to their Assessments as if they were the truth, instead of grounding them.

With my mom and the track meet, I didn't bother to "ground" my Assessment, so it shaped my life for decades. Imagine the difference it would have made if I'd had that conversation with her forty years earlier? The automatic Assessment that would always come up when I thought something I was going to do would be difficult would have been gone. I wouldn't have heard my internal voice saying to me, "Don't forget, you never have it when the going gets tough." Now if I hear that, I just find it interesting and then complete the task I am doing.

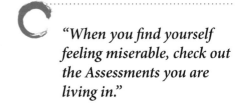

"When you find yourself feeling miserable, check out the Assessments you are living in."

LEARN FROM MY MISTAKE

The next time you find yourself in the swirl of Assessments regarding a specific moment in your life, it's useful to ask yourself, "Does this Assessment open up new possibilities for me or close them down?" Now you have the choice to keep it or let it go.

When you find yourself feeling miserable, check out the Assessments you are living in and that you believe are "The Truth." Explore the validity of your internal Assessments—or those others have made about you—and see just how grounded they are before you carry on.

THE FREEDOM ASSESSMENTS CAN GIVE US

As I said before, Assessments are personal opinions, judgments, and interpretations about how we, or others, feel or think about a specific subject matter. They are NEVER right or wrong, true or false. They are, however, either "grounded or ungrounded."

In the story above, my mother had never even said what I thought I heard. But what if she had said it, and meant it? That would have been a moment to personally ground her Assessments and begin a new story about how we can have a more meaningful relationship as we move into the future.

As we have been exploring, language shapes our world, relationships, and meaning in every moment. Freedom lives in our willingness to ask questions that generate clarity and understanding rather than right or wrong.

Many breakdowns come from listening to someone else's Assessments of us, as if they are fact. Spoken Assessments say more about the speaker than anyone else; they reflect the concern of the speaker who brings forth or is driving their Assessments. Listening for the background and concerns of people's Assessments—the foundational reasoning of the speaker for making certain statements—can be a powerful management tool, in business and in life.

> *"Many breakdowns come from listening to someone else's Assessments of us, as if they are fact."*

Asking the speaker what their concerns are about the situation allows them to get it off their chest and then be able to open a sound conversation. Once again it is about clarity and understanding first before making your Assessment.

But even when people make Assessments about us that we believe are true and grounded, we still have the opportunity to change our behavior—and their Assessments about us—by choosing new actions.

Other people's Assessments only have the power to haunt us and cut us off from opportunities if we let them. Knowing that they frequently say more about the person making them than they do about the person they are speaking of sets us free.

ASSESSING OTHERS

Just as other people's Assessments of us can cause us distress and missed opportunities—unless we become aware of them and learn to manage them—our Assessments of others can do lasting damage to their psyches and to the relationships we have with them as well.

ASSESSMENTS ARE THE WATER WE SWIM IN

Assessments are like water to a fish and air to a bird. If we could ask them how the water or the air is, they would answer, "What water?" "What air?" We are surrounded by our Assessments and almost never notice how they are the water we swim in.

To improve our communication skills and make more positive contributions to other people's lives, it's important to learn how to communicate our Assessments for what they are—our interpretations of a situation, not fact.

For example, instead of saying, "This situation is . . . ," or "The truth about you is . . . ," you could say, "My assessment of the situation is . . . ," or "My interpretation of what you said is . . . ."

By opening your conversations in this way, you shift the mood to one of openness and collaboration. Other people are more likely to listen to what you are saying as a possible interpretation, rather than trying to defend their point of view, or getting their feelings hurt and shutting down.

A good practice is to do your best to share with your friends new Assessments that have the opportunity to enhance your relationship. For example, "You seem so happy, and I would love to learn more of what is happening in your life that has given you this new outlook." Or when you are in a meeting or with another and you don't understand their point of view, try saying, "Tell me more about your assessment of the situation." And then open your reply with "My assessment is X. Does that make sense to you?"

In working toward understanding and alignment, just about everything is possible. When in doubt, try asking for clarity and understanding. It is the shortest path for grounding assessments.

Just remember: Assessments are our personal opinions and points of view, based on our own view of the world. When we are grounded in this interpretation of Assessments, and speak from that interpretation, there is a different sense of life.

The need to prove we are right or know the "truth" about things subsides, and we find ourselves in a more relaxed and productive way of living. After all, they are only our Assessments. We have the right to share them with others, but not to inflict them on others as fact.

QUESTIONS TO PONDER

Doing side of life:

1. *Can you identify any reoccurring long-standing Assessments in your life that have limited who you are Being over the years?*

2. *How have your Assessments of others impacted both your life and theirs in positive and/or negative ways? Do you see how you can leverage the positive assessments to create new futures?*

   Example: "I now have a new assessment of the situation that might shed additional light on things. Would you like to hear my new interpretations?"

3. *How can Assessments be a powerful tool in generating a positive future?*

QUESTIONS TO PONDER (CONT.)

Being side of life:

1. What new interpretations are you discovering about your awareness of the role Assessments play in your and others' lives?

2. With these new awarenesses, whom can you see your Self being that will allow you to live a more peaceful life?

   Example: I can now see my Self being a person who holds Assessments as opportunities to make new decisions in my life, not out of reaction but rather out of choice.

3. Who can you see your Self being if you allowed yourself to speak kindly of those around you and yourself? What new ways of being would you expect to see appearing for you and your world?

4. What if we knew we were always in the process of creating our world from the words we speak? What would your world begin to look like if you didn't blame anyone for anything, including yourself? Try this out and see what happens. Limiting blame of myself and others has made one of the most impactful shifts in my life. What I notice now is that very few people blame me for anything.

CHAPTER 8:
THE SWIRL, A PERFECT STORM OF LANGUAGE

*"We are not human beings having a spiritual experience;
we are spiritual beings having a human experience."*

PIERRE TEILHARD DE CHARDIN

We are all caught in the routine of the matrix, the uncertainty of the matrix, the confusion of the matrix, the absurdity of the matrix. This is the Linguistic Swirl in which we live.

I call this the "Perfect Storm of Living in Language." Understanding what creates this storm is the key to coming through it intact, rather than drowning at sea.

In the movie The Perfect Storm, George Clooney plays a fisherman in a small New England village who departs on a Grand Banks fishing trip with his rough-and-tumble crew.

At the same time, a nerdy Boston meteorologist is watching three different storms converge on one another—one from the north, one from the south, and another from the east. All of them would meet just over New England—a meteorological phenomenon that had never happened at this magnitude before. The now-terrified meteorologist starts broadcasting this weather occurrence as "the perfect storm," because he knew that when those storms collided, the atmosphere would be chaos, very similar to the 250-mile-per-hour typhoon that took place in the Philippines.

That film, and the book on which it was based, provided a great story and a powerful metaphor for me.

I call a section of the The Riff process The Perfect Storm because there are three powerful personal elements that live in that linguistic domain:

1. The Little Inner Voice

2. The role of the physical body, our Automaticity

3. Our Assessments

When we're influenced by one of them, life is interesting. When we're influenced by two of them, it gets a little unsettling. But when all three of these elements intermix, you can experience chaos. That's when you have one of those days when you wonder: "Where can I just stand still for a while? Where is the solid ground? Is there anything I can trust?"

When we are unaware of the Swirl created by The Perfect Storm of Living in Language, life can seem pretty chaotic. The little voice is screaming at us to either do this or do that. The body is responding to just about any trigger. And there's a vast variety of past personal Assessments floating around, further adding to the confusion.

The interesting thing about this situation is that these ingredients all came with your package. They helped shape you into who you are, and they can make your life better or cause you to have a nervous breakdown. Which way it goes depends on your awareness of them.

We all have given it our best shot with these three elements, and to some degree, most of us have learned to use them somewhat effectively. We are still here; we do have happy days, love, and laughter in our lives. That being said, becoming the Observer of these tools can give us new insights on how to use them as we move forward.

But when we're not aware of these elements, and the power they exert on our lives, and when all three converge on us at once, it can feel as if there is no escape. I'm sure you have heard the analogy of the lovely green frog, who when put in warm water with the ever-increasing high heat never recognizes that the water is starting to boil, thus ensuring his tragic demise. Sometimes we find ourselves feeling like that. Life gets more and more intense, more and more confusing, more and more threatening, one small bit at a time. Before we realize it, we're boiling.

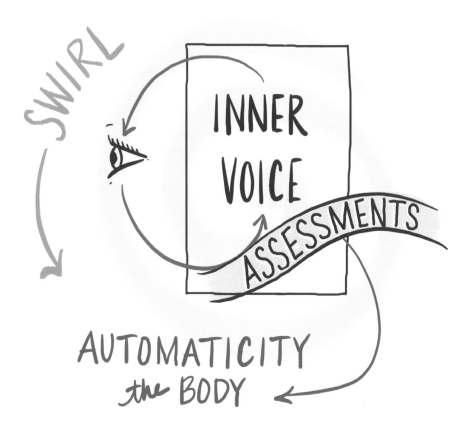

Most people consider themselves to be the Swirl. We have those three elements always moving around in such a way that we start to consider ourselves to be that Swirl. The interesting phenomenon here is that the Swirl can't be "who we are," because if it was, we couldn't talk about it. We would have no place from which to observe it.

"Most people consider themselves to be the Swirl. We have those three elements always moving around in such a way that we start to consider ourselves to be that Swirl."

SHIFT IN PERSPECTIVE EXERCISE

When I am at this point in a conversation about not being the Swirl, I often hold up my index finger on my right hand and ask my client if that finger could tell me what it looked like. My client ponders for a while, perplexed. The answer I assert is that it could not tell me what it looked like because it is all finger. Then I hold up my index finger on my left hand and ask, "If this left index finger could see and speak, could it tell the right finger what it looks like?" My client might then say, "Yes it could," and when I ask why, they could look at me and reply, "Because it can see the other finger from a different perspective."

Along this same line, I often think about the early cavemen. Since they had no mirrors they truly did not know what color eyes they had, it took another human outside their own body, or a pool of still water, to truly see the color. We are now intellectually sophisticated enough to perceive something other than our immediate outward perception; we can think in the abstract; we can imagine other realities.

RISE ABOVE THE SWIRL BY BECOMING AN OBSERVER

One way to avoid being consumed by the Swirl or letting it negatively impact you is to become the new bigger Observer of the way your world is occurring.

It is like watching a sporting event from the press box rather than playing in the game on the field. From the press box, you can see the entire game taking place. The pitcher throws the ball; the batter hits the ball; the center-fielder catches the ball.

From up above the Swirl of the game, you coach the pitcher to throw the ball to third base because you can see the runner is not stopping at second. You can clearly see what is happening, and anticipate what is about to happen, because you're seeing it all at once.

If you were a player on the field, you would see the pitcher throw the ball. After that, you'd start trying to figure out what you should do. You might lose sight of the ball or look to first base to see what the runner is going to do so you can decide if you should head toward third base. You'd be so focused on what comes next that you wouldn't be able to see all the moving pieces at once.

The opportunity here is to find a way to your own personal press box so that you can see what is happening at any given moment in your game called Life. It is not about trying to figure it out, but rather seeing how you and the players are moving around your field.

Viewing life from the press box, where you can be a new Observer, gives you the opportunity to not only see what is taking place at that moment but also to better determine what actions you can take that would allow you to move forward. When you can trust this deeper, richer

"When you can trust this deeper, richer outside voice, the Bigger Observer, a shift takes place, one that quiets the concerns of the moment."

outside voice, the New Observer, a shift takes place, one that quiets the concerns of the moment.

PAUL'S STORY: SURVIVING THE SWIRL

My client Paul came to me after he experienced a traumatic and life-threatening situation that almost cost him his well-being—and even his life. Paul is a fascinating person, engaged in making a difference as a corporate leadership coach as well as in working with veterans suffering from PTSD.

Paul grew up in Africa with his English parents and eventually started a safari company. He would take his clients on photo safari as well as river trips showing them the most amazing mixtures of landscape, wildlife, and the life that takes place in Africa every day. Paul's incident involved one of the days on a river trip and the danger that hippos offered anyone who came near their pod, especially the ones with young offspring.

It was one of those beautiful days on the Zambezi River, and when they paddled around the bend, the water rushed by and they saw a whole pod of hippos immediately before them. One of Paul's guides was leading the way, and Paul was in his kayak following, in the sweep role, to make sure everybody was taken care of. As they came around the turn, Paul saw one of the male hippos start to charge the canoe in the middle of the river.

He paddled as fast as he could to insert his kayak in between the charging hippo and the canoe, saving those people's lives. As he intercepted the charging hippo, the hippo grabbed him by his upper body and jerked him out of the kayak. After shaking him for what seemed to be an eternity, the hippo threw Paul out of its mouth only to turn around and this time pick him up with his entire upper body inside the hippopotamus' mouth.

Eventually the hippopotamus tried to hold Paul under the water long enough to drown him. Paul's memory of that moment was holding onto the tusks of the hippo, hearing water splashing around him, and wondering who was going to win the contest. Could the hippo hold Paul under the water longer than Paul could hold his breath?

Before the hippo once again threw Paul out of its mouth, its teeth had pierced both his lungs and almost torn off his arm. Paul was able to grab the handle on the end of another guide's kayak, enabling him to pull Paul away from the enraged hippopotamus.

Once they had cleared all danger and gotten Paul to the shore to administer first aid, they discovered what serious damage the hippo's jaws had done to Paul's physical body. Clearly there were no hospitals in the near vicinity, and there was likely no way to get Paul out of the area to any hospital for at least five more miles downriver.

Paul's fellow guide started administering first aid to the wounds on Paul's arms, shoulder, and chest. He eventually wound up wrapping plastic wrap around Paul's chest to seal the punctures that the hippopotamus had put in his lungs. He also administered general first aid as best he could, to enable them to continue down the river with Paul.

Paul would tell me that as he rode down the river in the bottom of the canoe, he heard himself saying, "I am not sure if I should be glad to be alive or if I should have died." Eventually they reached a helicopter landing zone, where an Army helicopter arrived to pick Paul up.

After an arduous helicopter ride and short drive to the hospital in a Jeep, he arrived at the emergency entrance. Paul recalled the stricken look on the doctor's face as he gazed down at his body. As the doctor said, "Let's get him into the operating room," Paul stopped them and asked the doctor if he thought he could save his life. The doctor looked at Paul, and after a short pause, he answered, "I think I can." Then he asked, "Paul, why do you ask?" And Paul answered, "Because if you can't save my life, let me die now."

The doctor determinedly committed to saving Paul's life and took him into the operating room. As you can imagine, the doctor did a miraculous job, and although physically handicapped, Paul is alive and well and living with his wife and family in Detroit, Michigan.

As he and I started to do The Riff together, I asked him to tell me his story, as I do with most everyone. When they ask me what story they should tell me, my answer is always the same: "The one you want to tell me."

It seems that when we listen and give people the opportunity to tell us their story, the one they usually choose is the one that means the most to them, either in their present life or during their past. Paul proceeded to tell me his version of that day on the Zambezi River. During his story there were times when he was quite touched that he is still here with us and that his present life is so astounding. And right next to those moments were the sadness and fears that he continued to live through as he recovered.

We moved through The Riff, and Paul continued to discover how amazing it was that after all those years, the same old stories made his body respond with the same sensations that he had experienced in the real-time moment. As we said, in the Swirl, your Little Inner Voice can say something that triggers the body's Automaticity into somewhat the same body sensations it recalls from the real-time moment. Then we have our Assessments that try to support us in living through this reinterpretation of that moment in real time.

As Paul started to see the story from outside the Swirl, he noticed that his body was calming down and becoming more relaxed and the

Assessments that he'd had started to shift from "Oh, my gosh; isn't that horrible?" to "Isn't that interesting? I've never seen it that way before." As we continued through the various conversations about what he was discovering, he started to notice not only that his body was much more relaxed but also that his internal conversation, or Little Inner Voice, had become very silent—a silence you could feel in the room and see in his face.

He asked me what had just happened and why it was so quiet. I said, "Paul, it is an interesting moment in this part of The Riff. Just about every time I do this with people, they notice that their world becomes quiet and things that seemed to bother them in the past have lost their impact. Instead of trying to figure it out, why don't we just linger in this silence and let it seep in?"

"Living at peace is one's ability to traffic from inside the Swirl to outside the Swirl, where you are a new Observer."

The next morning when Paul came in for breakfast, he had a big grin on his face. I said, "Tell me what is happening?" He said that for the first time since that day on the river, being in the hippo's jaws, he had not seen those images in his eyes. He shared his amazement that by just being able to see it from outside the Swirl, it seemed there was now a place to go that would give him peace.

THE NEW VOICE OF THE BIGGER OBSERVER

Living at peace is one's ability to traffic from inside the Swirl to outside the Swirl, where you are a new Observer. It's an instinctual phenomenon.

Let's say you're working really hard on a project, and it's not progressing as you would have liked. You have tried everything, including working harder and harder, until you finally decide to give up or quit.

What's the last thing your body does before you say, "I quit"? It instinctively takes a deep breath, in and out, and for a moment everything seems to slow down or stop. In that moment, things don't seem so hopeless, and out of nothing comes this deeper, richer voice that says, "Here; do this." You do it, and things begin to move again. Or it might say, "This will work out; just let go."

This Bigger Observer voice tells you it will all work out, or to keep going, or to trust the process. If you listen you might hear it suggest a new action. Then you take this new action, and what happens? Things lighten up and you naturally see the path to follow.

At this moment, your need to figure things out can be transformed into a willingness to just "trust the Force, Luke." When you trust yourself to take those actions, you see life as a series of new openings, where you can have more peacefulness and more opportunities to be the Self that you don't know yourself to be. The need to prove yourself seems to slip away, and your actions begin to fall into alignment with who you have always known you are. You can, simply put, just "Be," and let things "Be."

This deeper, richer voice of the Bigger Observer is what we need to focus on, talk about. Why? Because that voice lives outside the Swirl. It sees life without all those Assessments, all the Automatic actions of the body, and most of all without the disruptive internal dialogue of the Little Inner Voice.

Fortunately, accessing the bigger voice of the new Observer and shifting out of the Swirl may be as easy as taking a deep breath. I think this is why almost all awareness training or meditations, or even swinging a golf club, are always preceded by taking a deep breath. Sometimes it's instinctual; sometimes it's intentional.

We are continually instructed to "breathe consciously" in yoga class. Breathing consciously is the essence of yoga, as it assists us in connecting with the subtle energy within. It is through the breath that we are able to navigate different levels of consciousness. Moreover, breathing consciously has a biological effect on our mental, emotional, and physical state. It brings you into the present; you let go of the past and future and are focused on the moment inside the breath.

Helpful Hint: To traffic outside of the Swirl, just breathe. Your body will fall into its comfort zone. Magically, the breath takes the Swirl away.

"A yogi measures the span of life by the number of breaths, not by the number of years."

Swami Sivananda

When you breathe consciously, you also activate a different part of your brain. Unconscious breathing is controlled by the medulla oblongata in the brain stem, the primitive part of the brain, while conscious breathing comes from the more evolved areas of the brain in the cerebral cortex. Consciously breathing sends impulses from the cortex to the connecting areas that impact emotions, which has a relaxing and balancing effect on the emotions.

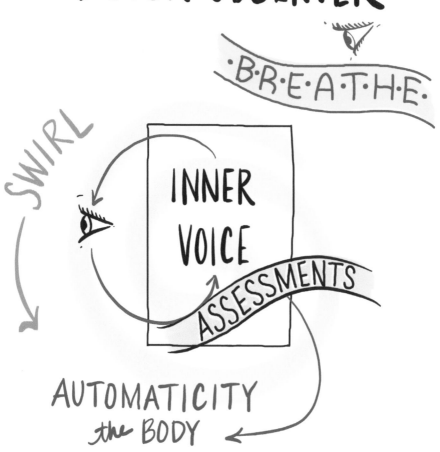

In essence, by consciously breathing, you are controlling which aspects of the mind dominate, causing your consciousness to rise from the primitive/instinctual to the evolved/elevated.

When we do breathe in this way, the world seems to stop for a moment and we can see things from outside the Swirl. Suddenly, we are aware of new actions to take, as well as what new actions not to take. The Little Voice quiets down and falls into alignment because it has recovered its comfort zone and finds nothing to yell about.

LIVING IN THE SWIRL

Once people discover their natural ability to observe their Swirl, it seems to lose its power and actually can become an asset. We can move in and out of the Swirl at will, empowering us to weather the storms—while also learning from them.

As I walked in to our kitchen after returning from a two-day meeting I had been leading in Pittsburgh, Judy knew from my facial expression that it had been a tough couple of days. While the meeting turned out well for everyone concerned, I found myself presently in a deep mood of sadness caused by being reminded how, from time to time, people treat each other so poorly, without kindness and respect. During this meeting, people frequently said incredibly negative things about each other and to each other, which caused unneeded sadness and resentment. Their personal Swirl limited any larger vision or compassion.

I told Judy I was just sad that the group I was working with had to go through that unneeded interaction while on their way to building increased trust amongst themselves.

Judy asked me if there was anything she could do to support me with that sadness. "No," I said. "I'm going to stay in this Swirl of sadness intentionally to see how it will unravel itself and what I can learn from it."

After a couple of days, the sadness disappeared. At that moment I wanted to go back and try to figure out what had happened to make it disappear, but I didn't. I just acknowledged that it had, and I seemed to be back in the flow of life.

That experience provided a really impactful lesson for me. Sometimes, if you leave something like that alone, it will run out of energy on its own and disappear.

My new mantra when I find myself in the Swirl is to say, "Isn't that interesting," and take no action. Trying to stop it, fix it, or change it may only prolong it. An old metaphysical adage says "What you resist persists," so I am in the swing of observing—letting go and trusting life will unfold just the way it is supposed to.

When I find myself in the Swirl, a positive action is to say, "Isn't that interesting," and to take no action.

I'm not saying to run away and hide from it; I am saying there is real power in observing it. Then, if needed, you can listen to your New Bigger Observer voice, take the actions it recommends, and see what happens.

People often share with me that once they learn about being inside the Swirl and then listening to their New Observer, they find that when they say to themselves "Isn't that interesting? I'm in the Swirl," they then almost instantaneously find themselves outside of it and observing life from a new perspective. It is as if they were a CBS sports announcer describing what the next plays are on the field.

In order to live a more peaceful life, the goal is to be able to shift from inside the Swirl to outside the Swirl by simply acknowledging it. From that perspective, the next step is to observe what is taking place, breathe, and simply ask the new Bigger Observer a question, like "Let me see?" then wait for the deeper voice to respond. When it responds, take the actions it suggests, and if there is no response, then do not take any actions.

A caution: If you are in immediate danger in the Swirl, take yourself out. The new Bigger Observer will give you fresh insight when you are out of your Automaticity. If there is no response, then leave that situation alone and there might be a good chance that it will go away. Sometimes I think that most of the problems we try to fix don't need fixing at that moment and might go away if you leave them alone. We are all unique people, so see how this might work for you.

MANAGING MOMENTS OF SADNESS AND CHANGE

My daughter's friend Janet was living in Europe when she called me for advice after a major breakdown with her long-time boyfriend. We discussed her situation at length—the complexity of living abroad, what her next steps might be, and if and how to maintain her relationship.

I told her, "I am sorry for all the pain you are going through because of this separation. The body will eventually burn through the loss as it sees other places to find comfort. One way to slow down the Swirl is to manage how you speak about what you perceive this moment to look like. Is your speaking opening up new possibilities for your future or closing them down?"

When "life" happens, ask your Bigger Observer this simple question: "Let me see?" If you don't get a response, then don't take any action. If you do, then follow it and see what happens.

No matter how dark the moment might seem, there is always a way to share your interpretation that will open up new possibilities. You have a choice. You can say, "My life is horrible, and I don't see any way out." Or you can say, "My life seems to be in a 'moment' of change, and I am doing my best to find the right path as I continue to move forward."

This process is about describing what actions are taking place, much like an artist is capturing his or her interpretation of the world in that instant. The artist knows that the moment will not last forever, and neither will the sadness or stress you're dealing with during tough times.

There are days when I get up in a great mood, ready to soar. Yet, as my day unfolds, there don't seem to be any parking spaces where I need them, which makes me late to my meeting, and I get a parking ticket because I didn't see the street-cleaning signs.

I can either give up and say, "Life sucks, and nobody loves me," or I can say, "Isn't that interesting? I thought my day was going to be different."

This kind of statement seems to neutralize the situation while at the same time leaving you at a moment of choice—to keep moving forward or to stop and complain, which ultimately doesn't really accomplish anything.

Labeling the moment you find yourself in, at that instant, rather than labeling yourself as being that, is a powerful way to move.

Example: When you declare "I am depressed," in the moment of speaking, you find yourself becoming that persona and taking the actions your interpretation of the word "depressed" sees you taking. Over our lifetime, we have unconsciously programed ourselves to be who we are saying we are, in the moment of saying it: I am happy, I am sad, I don't like broccoli, I love X, I hate X, etc. If we can become aware of those types of declarations and learn to describe the moment we find ourselves in, then life becomes a series of interesting moments rather than a long-term story we find ourselves living.

"Over our lifetime, we have unconsciously programed ourselves to be who we are saying we are, in the moment of saying it."

One could say we live in a series of Moments that take place in our awareness, and if we just describe that Moment, then we also find ourselves at a time of choice to shift our awareness and to create words that can align with who we know ourselves to be.

Finding ourselves in Moments of our lives, we have a choice. By labeling ourselves with "I am ...," we are destined to exhibit those qualities. By saying "Isn't that interesting? It seems that I am in a moment of surprise. I thought I was going to find a parking space right here, and there wasn't one. Let's see, where will be the next parking space that I can park in?" we acknowledge that choice.

Another example might be "In this moment I find myself thinking that 'A' was going to happen and 'C' happened instead. Now let's see what is wanting to happen next."

It is called the dance of life; enjoy it.

The "next" moment holds within itself all imaginable possibilities.

In these moments, I find it much more useful to ask my Bigger Observer this simple question: **"What actions do you see I could be taking?"** If you don't get a response, then don't take any actions. If you do get a response, then follow them and see what happens.

ASSESSMENTS ARE THE WATER WE SWIM IN

Here's a great way to become the listener of the Bigger Observer's voice: For one week, when you are driving in heavy traffic and hear your Inner Little Voice say, "Go to the left lane," and then you hear your deeper New Observer voice say, "Go right," then go right. Most of us seem to do the exact opposite of our deeper voice and then sit in the left lane watching the right lane go whizzing by.

I have tested this in my own life and found that the Bigger Observer voice is right almost all the time. Why wouldn't it be telling you the accurate things to do when it is outside the Swirl, observing? We already have another voice trying to tell us what it thinks we should do from inside the Swirl. The life you want might just be as simple as listening to the Bigger Observer's voice –rather than trying to understand why the Little Inner Voice is saying what it's saying.

Eventually, your Little Inner Voice may find a way to trust your Observational voice and know it has found a safe place to see the world. When this happens, the Little Inner Voice quiets down and only acts up when it senses something dangerous is about to occur or doesn't understand what is about to happen. It even seems like the two voices have become one, and with that comes the peacefulness to live in our world knowing that this trust will always be with us.

LEAVING THE PAST IN THE PAST

Some of the most confusing and frustrating conversations we have are when we want to have a meaningful dialogue about something that happened in the past. If we don't manage it well, we find ourselves in the middle of a conversation that mixes up the past with the present and even touches the future. There is a good chance that this conversation will generate more problems than existed before. It is then that we find ourselves in the middle of the Swirl.

One solution is to declare when you are speaking about the past, when you are speaking about the present, and when you are speaking about the future. At times all three of those areas of our awareness seem to turn into one big clump of time, and the listener doesn't know what you are talking about. In order to avoid this condition, I suggest stating the time frame you are speaking about in that moment.

Let's say you would like to talk about something that happened a year ago that had an impact on your relationship, and you would like to have a conversation about it now and share your present interpretation.

You can start by saying, "In the past, I would have said X about this situation. Now I would say Y about the situation, which gives me a new sense of a greater future that is beginning to unfold, and in the future I could see myself saying Z." All three statements are valid in representing your present interpretation. The usefulness of this type of approach is that if they begin to drift into the clump again, you can clarify which time frame you are referring to, which will maintain the focus of the conversation.

This approach also works well when you are having a professional conversation with a coworker who you may be managing.

Let's say they come to you for your advice about a decision you will have to make about their career. At that moment, you realize that you have several types of relationships with this coworker: your professional one, your personal friendship one, your coworker one, and others.

So your answer could sound something like this: "As your boss I would say you should do A; as your friend I would say you should do B; and as your coworker I would say you should do C." All of these responses are accurate answers in their respective domains. At the same time, they maintain the clarity of who you are speaking on behalf of and the respective relationship you have with the listener.

When the interaction is compartmentalized like this, the listener can track the flow and keep things separated. There is also clarity in the body's comfort zone, because it isn't dealing with fear from the past and therefore can start taking actions to have its vision for the future become real.

I suggest that we spend 90 percent of our brains' everyday bandwidth managing the past, which puts us smack in the middle of the Swirl and our societal matrix. That only leaves us 10 percent for seeing what

"I suggest that we spend 90 percent of our brains' everyday bandwidth managing the past."

RECORD YOURSELF

Everything we have been talking about in this book relates to how our lives live in the language we are speaking, listening, or imagining. For that reason, I suggest you start recording conversations you are having around breakdowns—not to listen to how bad things are, but to listen for new ways of speaking which will allow you to intentionally design a new way of Being in your ever-shifting world.

This practice of recording your conversations gives you an opportunity to hear whether your conversations are opening possibilities or closing them down. I suggest you be especially mindful of whether you are using "Being" words or "Doing" words. Being words seem to open possibilities, and the Doing words seem to close them down. The shift could be as easy as saying could instead of should, might instead of will, and have happen instead of want.

the future holds. But when you are accessing your New Observer, the past shifts and exists in a different way than it did before. This is a space you can naturally fall back to because you're not consuming your life predominantly in the past; you're actually living it in the present, a life where you can make the contribution that you came here to make and where there is an opportunity to be the Self that you don't yet know yourself to be.

Remember: You are not the Swirl; you are the Observer of the Swirl. From up above and outside the Swirl, you have the chance to notice that most of the conversations going on in your head are from the past and offer no new possibilities. They simply keep you going around in circles.

Even in circumstances that may seem unresolvable, stepping outside the Swirl is possible. For example, my client Andy, a Chief Technology Officer was involved in a serious car accident where his best friend died. Understandably, the incident left him traumatized for years and with an ongoing internal conversation that limited him from living a peaceful and inspired life. There was a powerful moment when we were doing The Riff where something shifted and he was able to see a new way to live, to step outside the Swirl to create a new interpretation of the incident and get his life back.

When you listen to the stories as if they are really about you—the "little you" in the Swirl—there is a tendency to drift into a hopeless mindset. But if you just observe it as some internal chatter grounded in nothing and let it pass on by, there is a good chance it will lose its power. If it comes back again, it should have less impact on you. Then you can ask yourself, "What is the best way to move forward?" and "Isn't that interesting?"

If you find yourself back in the Swirl, acknowledge it, and shift to your Bigger Observer. Give yourself some room to see another way to move and to be the Self that you don't know yourself to be.

"You are not the Swirl; you are the Observer of the Swirl."

QUESTIONS TO PONDER

Doing side of life:

1. *When you look back over what you have read, what aspects do you see have made the most sense to you, and how do you see you could use them in living a more peaceful lifestyle?*

2. *What are the best new practices you could design that would support you in being the observer of when you are in and outside the Swirl? What reward could you see yourself using to reinforce these new observations?*

Being side of life:

1. *Do you see how you can be in the Swirl and in the next moment become your Outside Observer just by acknowledging that you are in it?*

2. *How do you see yourself shifting from one to the other? Shifting is like a muscle; it needs to be used.*

3. *Who do you see yourself Being when you are not in the Swirl, and what new ways of being does that offer you in your day-to-day life?*

4. *What new ways of Being are you seeing appear around you that are contributing to your life? Please set a section in your journal for logging these discoveries.*

CHAPTER 9:
THE SHIFT

"Vision is the art of seeing things invisible."

JONATHAN SWIFT

This book has been fundamentally about how to live in the Being side of life. When you do that, you amplify your Self. In today's matrix, we may find life being wired up backwards. We were brought up to DO a bunch of things to find out later if our Being can fit into that world. I suggest we live life the other way around, where we win the game first and then play it.

If you have a vision of the future, and then a vision of yourself inside that vision, and you start to align with that vision, the world falls into alignment with you and your actions. In other words, when you're clear on who you can see yourself Being in the future, all your actions fall into alignment with that outcome, so what you're Doing is in alignment with who you can see yourself Being.

"When you're clear on who you can see yourself Being in the future, all your actions fall into alignment with that outcome."

Exceptional sports teams and athletes approach their competitions that way. There's been a lot of documentation about how "visioning" an

Olympic downhill ski run, a final tennis match, or a championship golf game improves performance. I've had that experience myself rowing competitively in the Head of the Charles Regatta and Sprints. Many of you may have read the bestselling book Boys in the Boat, which beautifully details the life of a Washington state farm boy who ends up surviving the Depression and rowing in the Olympics in Nazi Germany. That compelling story is all about envisioning your future and being true to yourself.

A letter to my client Justin from me:

Dear Justin,

Thanks for our last couple of calls. I find it exciting to hear your burning desire to have your art recognized in the world; the message is loud and clear, and very different than before. While your Self is still in the conversation, it is being led by a vision that is calling on its greatness to be realized rather than the story of its greatness to be recognized. That outer recognition will occur in a moment of peace when you allow the world to join in as a true partner, rather than as a hurdle to clear.

As we have discussed in the past, the "Art of Allowing" occurs when you are ready to see that the world is in alignment with the vision it is drawing you towards. It is about allowing yourself to be used "by the Force, Luke;" that opens the world to join in, allowing the flow to unfold naturally. When this happens, each action seems to be in step with the natural unfolding of what is wanting to happen. Effort seems to fall by the wayside and accomplishment leads the way.

My recommendation, Justin, is to simply breathe, stay the course, and be aware of what the world is offering as guidance in this moment of your journey. You'll be amazed.

As you are discovering, most of the misinterpretations in our lives happen as the result of reacting to our world, rather than just observing the actions that are taking place. Once you see your actions as a New Observer, you find yourself able to move with the flow of life at any moment, rather than trying to direct the flow or resist it.

I suggest the world has a bigger idea for you and your actions than you will ever figure out. This new game is to see the "offers" the world is making you without having to change anything. The interesting aspect of the world's offers is that they are in complete alignment with you and your abilities, so there is nothing else to DO, just allow yourself to BE you. It comes down to a series of simple choices for you to make. One choice at a time.

Warmly,

Joel

All along, the world has been offering each of us new openings to move on naturally in our lives. We've recognized some of those opportunities as "strokes of luck," and perhaps passed on some of them because they seemed "too good to be true." Others we haven't even noticed, because we were too busy Doing and managing our past.

Someone once said, "Listen to the whispers, and when you do, those sounds begin to draw you in that direction." My interpretation: "We have been busting it to make something happen, and now may be the time to just allow what is wanting to happen to happen."

TIME FOR A PLAYBACK

We've covered a lot of ground in this book, so now let's review The Riff process, realizing that the new Bigger Observer allows you to separate yourself from the Swirl of the game and move to the "art" of the sport.

The Riff process is about rising above the Swirl. This means becoming aware of the three elements that make up the Perfect Storm of Living in Language:

1. **The Little Inner Voice:** The "internal conversations" we have with ourselves were formed right from the beginning of our lives. The uncertainty of the intent behind what the Little Voice is saying seems to keep us second-guessing whether what we are doing is right or wrong. This internal conversation shapes the way our world occurs to us. This is simply part of being human and can be expected in all aspects of life. The goal is not to try to stop the Little Voice, but rather to allow it to rattle along like "talk radio," playing in the background while you stay focused on what you're intending to accomplish and on whom you see yourself Being.

2. **The Body:** The body is triggered into action by just about anything it comes in contact with. "WATCH OUT!!!" automatically makes the body cringe and look around to see if there is danger. This "Automaticity" of the body seems to happen unconsciously and starts the whole process of our minds trying to make order of things and figure out what is happening. We all have our own Automaticities, and we are dealing with everyone else having theirs. But as you become an Observer of your Automaticity, you can manage those dynamics from choice rather than from habit.

3. **The Assessments:** These stories we've made up throughout our lifetimes—both in our own minds and by listening to the Assessments of others—show up as if they are the truth, when in fact they may not be. Assessments either open up new possibilities for

us or close them down. Once we become aware of the Assessments that we are living in and that have shaped our lives thus far, we can see new choices and actions to take when these same Assessments reappear.

4. **The Perfect Storm:** As the body's Automaticity impacts our internal conversations, so do our Assessments. All three of these elements are interrelated, and if one is triggered into action, it often calls the others into action as well, generating the Perfect Storm of Living in Language and keeping us trapped in the Linguistic Swirl, where we don't have a clear view of the big picture of our lives.

Through language, we form a matrix or hologram of life in which we live. The opportunity is to learn the skill of shifting from that matrix to a new observation point, thus becoming your outside New Observer.

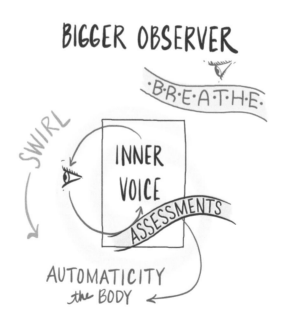

READY TO CHANGE YOUR TUNE? OR HOW THE RIFF CAME TO BE.

When you become an adept Observer, "change" is a matter of performing new actions rather than trying to change who you are or who you have been. Here are some fun things to try.

1. Write a journal and observe it.

2. Begin to listen to your conversations, both the ones you are speaking out loud and your internal conversations you are having with yourself.

3. Sit and Observe the thoughts you are having, and notice the predominant conversations/ stories you are presently living in.

"You'll find your body is more peaceful when you are Outside. There's no sensation of angst or uncertainty. That's how you know you're there."

The Bigger Observer observes our actions while we are living in the Swirl. This Observer is always there; we just need to access it by intentionally taking a deep breath in and out. It allows us to step back and see life from a more expansive perspective; then we can live life from choice rather than Automaticity.

On the left is an exercise that my clients have found helpful for working their new muscle of becoming an Outside Observer.

One of my clients asked, "How do I know if I'm outside this Swirl or still in it?" My simple answer: You'll find your body is more peaceful when you are outside. There's no sensation of angst or uncertainty when you are outside looking in. The world could be in chaos around you, but if you take a breath and go, "Well, let's see . . . ," all of a sudden your body will breathe, and the world around you will stop momentarily so you can see what's being revealed. That moment where you can see with a new eye after a deep breath—that's where you listen not to the internal, cynical, and fearful Inner Voice but for that Bigger Observer voice.

On the other hand, if you find yourself tense, with a stiff neck, grinding your teeth, clutching your hands, or tightening whatever part of your body in which you tend to hold your tension, you can almost be positive you are functioning inside the Swirl.

What is the next move? Take a breath, feel the release, and focus on your vision—who you can see your "self" Being, rather than what you should be Doing. Then bring your language into alignment with that lush, enthralling vision and take action.

As you launch into your new journey of living outside the Swirl and Being the person you can see yourself being, make sure you take the time to acknowledge your "Self" and your body by name for all that it is doing to allow you to fulfill your vision, the world, and those around you.

Using your body's name when making the acknowledgement allows the body and the Self to take those new actions.

One night I woke up and realized that what was supposed to happen, happens and what is not supposed to happen, doesn't happen. With that insight I found myself wondering what there was really to worry about. As my mother said, worrying doesn't get you anywhere.

You have my deepest thanks for taking the time to read this book and for seeing what is available if we just allow ourselves to be part of the solution, to live a rich and full life that will continue to unfold in alignment with the Vision we have for ourselves.

As I was told by one of my mentors, "Everything you will ever need is everywhere always. All you need to do is ask and SEE how it is given."

I'd like to end this book by leaving you with a sense of what's possible. Life can be a magical event; it can be a dance with the matrix, a sumptuous feast for our Self, and a wonderful game to play. Like any game you play, you don't always win, but one thing you can be sure of: If you practice, you get better, and you can discover your power of Self.

Hopefully this book has given you lots of food for thought, and even some moments of sheer inspiration. I'd like to end on a high note by encouraging you to keep dancing, play with language, enjoy each day, appreciate your Self, and be curious. When you see new ways to use these insights, pause and make a note on how you can see them Being part of your vibrant new life—and then dance onward.

As Buckminster Fuller would say, *You never change things by fighting the existing reality. To change something, build a new model that makes the existing model obsolete.*

"*The state of trusting yourself to trust yourself is where the magic lives in life.*"

QUESTIONS TO PONDER

Doing side of life:

1. Are you starting to notice yourself shifting from your Swirl to the Bigger Observer? If so, which focus do you see as the most supportive perspective?

2. Out of these new insights, what are you willing to allow to happen for yourself that you would not allow before?

3. Can you envision yourself shifting in and out of your Swirl and the matrix to gain insight and personal freedom? Log three new discoveries of how incidents and circumstances are beginning to support you in fulfilling your vision rather than causing frustration.

Being side of life:

1. Allow your Self to know that what is shifting in your life from what you have learned while reading this book is what is supposed to be shifting. New interpretations and awareness can lead to new and more natural ways of Being in your world.

2. Seeing these new insights as openings and ideas rather than things to do is powerful. Keep jotting them down.

ACKNOWLEDGEMENTS

Acknowledgment is one of my core values, so it is not surprising to realize that I have a huge community of friends, professionals and family that I want to recognize in this first book. They have led me and pushed me to be a good team player, a smarter consultant and personal coach, a wiser listener, a caring father, all in all, I think, a better person. I dedicate this work to all those who have given me the gifts of Being that have allowed me to be the person I find myself to be in this very moment. While people do many things for us along the way, I suggest that what lasts the longest and has the largest impact is the sentiment and who they are being for you in the moment of interaction. Below are small groupings of those who have and will continue to make a difference in who I am in the world.

Frist Judy Addicott Kimmel my amazing wife, who taught me what is possible when someone comes from one's unconditional love and knows that things will always work out. She radiates the joy and beauty of life and being with others, and lives what it is to be a brilliant business partner, mother and friend, and an unending resource for our two beautiful thriving daughters.

Our two daughters, Emily and Whitney who provided the test ground for much of our work and who have proven to be radiant, successful, grounded women in their own right. They make my day. Ed and Lon Kimmel, my brothers and partners in all the adventures adolescence provides.

My Mom, Evelyn Kimmel-Taylor originally Canadian and proud of it, she was a genuine humanitarian. I honor her for living her life as a gift and never finding negative words to say about anyone. "Dig in boys, we are in Hog Heaven now" was her mantra while serving us dinner when we had little if any money to buy food.

Dad, Joseph Kimmel, a pilot and dreamer was an energy to be reckoned with, living by honoring and respecting others for living their life the best they can. "Yes mam" and "No mam", "Yes sir" and "No sir" was required for everyone when they addressed my brothers and me or asked us something. I still find myself occasionally saying that to younger people, it brings a smile to their face and mine as well.

Ken and Jane Addicott, Judy's parents. They both taught me the true joy of being in service to another's natural brilliance and they demonstrated that value every day, in every interaction, in every condition life presented.

A snap shot memory of "Jane Jane" as I called her, was of her sitting in the morning sun on her 100th birthday when Whitney and Emily started musing with her about her secrets to life. When they asked what was the secret of having a good relationship, Jane thought for a few moments and then she said, "Learn to count to 10". And we all laughed, yet you could see that she was still thinking about her response, then she looked at the girls and said in a drawn out voice "Very SLOOOWLY". Our girls talk about that guidance often as well as the most quoted response she gave to the question about her secret to longevity. Jane thought for a moment about it and said "Everything in moderation. Food, alcohol, hard work etc. and yet remember love and kindness are unlimited".

Her husband Dr. Ken Addicott was an extraordinary man who spent most of his life working at one of the highest levels of our government. In his career although continually stressful, there was never a question of whether he liked his responsibilities but rather the honor to be part of efforts that were making our country safer. His worldview was always engaged and historically enlightening. One of the enduring gifts I received from Ken was his appreciation that in a time of stress or crisis it takes all concerned to work together to reach an alignment and understanding, developing a resolution that addresses everyone's interests and reveals each participant's role in being part of a solution. The world needs more of this inspiration.

Beyond my parents and wife and dear family and friends of many years that are too many to mention, some people I would like to note and thank for their wisdom and insight. From my childhood and early adult life, Bob Feller; Grandfather Walton; Staff Sargent William McNaer – boot camp; Norm Moffat Sr.; Wilford Houghton; Hap Ridgeway, the man who saved my life; Col. Ray Kamp – Retired Army Combat veteran; lifelong friends Bob Clasen; Dick and Sheila Morse, Norm Moffat Jr., Michael Weaber.

From my career and later life, Fernando Flores – master of Linguistics and Ontology; Werner Erhard – human potential guru; Jim Bergquist; John Yokoyama; Chris Majer; James Flaherty; Chauncey Bell; Rick Scott; Carrie Schwab Pomerantz; Ross Perot, Jr.; Carl Sewell; Lynne and Bill Twist; Lee and Marc Lesser; Liza and Raz Ingrasci, Roy Williams and Amy Castoro – The Williams Group; Angela Beissel; Diane and Landon Carter; Alan Collenette; Steve Johnson; and so many more.

ABOUT JUDY AND JOEL

Joel Kimmel is a leading expert in ontological design and how it impacts individuals, high-performance teams, and corporations. He has focused his career on building teams, organizations, and individuals, grounded in efficient, powerful, and effective communication technology. His promise to individual clients is that they will experience the benefits of personal creativity, an intimate sense of community, and an expanded commitment to building honest and authentic relationships in careers and personal lives.

His consulting has included start-ups and long-term management of viable, successful businesses, franchises, and international organizations. Joel's diverse background includes being a retail business owner, keynote speaker, business consultant, executive consultant, individual mentor, world-class athlete, Vietnam veteran, and the recipient of the Presidential Call to Service Award.

Joel has worked with numerous high-performance consulting firms including Turning Point Inc., BizFutures, Sportsmind, The Williams Group, The Human Potential Project, and others. He has extensive experience leading corporate trainings, consulting on problem solving, team intervention, and coaching individuals on personal performance and authentic action. Joel is an experienced one-on-one coach for executives and their teams as well as working with executives during times of career or corporate transition focusing on Innovation, Identity, and Design.

Joel's coaching has encompassed a broad spectrum of life, from corporate executives to outreach programs for inner-city youth. His clients include such noted businesses as US Bank, Shell Oil, Wells Fargo Wealth Legacy Group, Mattamy Corporation, Itron International, the Charles Schwab Foundation, Allianz Life, and many others. His perspective, whether as a keynote speaker or a personal coach, brings a fresh new approach to individual and corporate change. Joel currently lives joyously in the San Francisco Bay Area with his wife, Judy.

Judy Kimmel, mother of their two grown daughters and wife of Joel, grew up exploring the world and living in various countries throughout her father's diplomatic career. She spent her earlier life working in the areas of education, marketing, personal growth, and transformative management. Her career encompasses the fields of elementary education, retail and franchise management, business coaching, and nonprofit organizational expansion and strategy. Being an accomplished artist and avid rower, she has a unique, creative perspective on life.

Judy has played strategic roles in Hawken Day School, in Supercuts Corporation as franchisee and marketing consultant, in Primo's Coffee Company as owner of eleven retail locations, and in Kimmel & Company as consultant and coach. Her nonprofit engagement includes The est Foundation, the Beyond War Foundation, The Peace Alliance, and the Marin Rowing Association, establishing and expanding their outreach and national impact. She has been featured in Inc. magazine, MARIN magazine, and CBS 60 Minutes Bay Area and is the Recipient of the Marin County Democratic Peacebuilder Award.

Her passion will always be coaching and inspiring good management in the public sector as well as serving on a number of different nonprofit boards. Judy is dedicated to expanding understanding and fostering powerful yet nurturing relationships within her family, her community, and business partners.

Joel and Judy invite your comments at www.KimmelandCompany.com.

COMMENTS ON OUR WORK AND THIS BOOK

*"Thank you for your coaching and friendship over these years.
You have inspired and influenced me deeply."*

MICHAEL COLE
PRESIDENT OF US BANK ASCENT
PRIVATE CAPITAL MANAGMENT

*"Thank you, thank you! I just wanted to share with you that the
discontentment I described on the phone is gone. All of a sudden, the
feeling of discontent over what is not happening in my life was replaced
with this deep well of contentment and gratitude for the fact that I can
just relax into what IS happening and just continue to listen, observe
and follow it. And as long as I do that, I will be guided toward
what and who I am meant to be."*

JASON SWAIN
GONZAGA UNIVERSITY

*"I cannot put into words the depth of Joel's presentation.
It was a journey deep into the SELF. Joel has that something special
thing going on that cannot be described adequately through language
—you must experience it yourself."*

KRISTIN COATES
COATES CONSULTING

*"The team thrives on your positive presence and
your ability to make boats move."*

DUSTIN KRAUS, LEAD MEN'S COACH
MARIN ROWING ASSOCIATION

*I'm feeling myself just wanting to Be and not do—
which I think is a good thing.*

*I've already caught myself a couple of times going back in
to the swirl, but was able to see it and get back out. Powerful stuff.
I will keep you updated but I feel the shift already.*

ANNE BENOIST, MD. AND ACUPUNCTURIST

Comments

"I just finished re-reading your notes from June 10, 2010—WOW!!!
They are like fine wine. The guidance only gets better with time."

CARL SEWELL,
AUTHOR OF BESTSELLER CUSTOMERS FOR LIFE
CHAIRMAN, SEWELL AUTOMOTIVE

"I see the potential that is in front of me,
I see the opportunities, and I can engage in and envision
conversations that set my life on an exciting and
fulfilling path. If you were here Joel I would hug you; words to
not do it justice. Excited for what is infront of me."

ANDY DULKA
CHIEF INFORMATION OFFICER
REGIS CORPORATION

"Joel Kimmel's teaching is easy to understand and yet profound. It
reminded me to remove myself from the fray of the internal non-stop
messaging of a lifetime, of the shoulds and should-nots, and to step
outside the usual chatter of my mind into a quieter, less stressful place of
observation and peace. To remain there is the quest for me."

CAROLE ANGERMEIR,
FOUNDER CROSS CULTURAL JOURNEYS

"Integrating being and doing, with grit and wisdom shines through in Joel Kimmel's wonderful book, grounded in a lifetime of experience in guiding, teaching, living, and loving."

MARC LESSER,
AUTHOR, PRES. ZBA ASSOCIATES

"My personal climb from despair and pointlessness to vigor, optimism and a lust for life are based entirely on Joel's teaching of the language, the words that inhabit the inner voice and that can be taught to focus on possibilities instead of on pointlessness.

The language was taught to me through an encounter with this magical man who possesses sincerity, selflessness and quiet certainty, all born of prior unthinkable personal pain and trauma. His overwhelming gift to me has been the ability to translate for me the untranslatable, abstract, ways in which the language, chosen subjectively and deliberately by the mind, interacts with the soul in the way that a teacher (kind or otherwise) interacts with her impressionable students."

ALAN COLLENETTE
EXECUTIVE REGIONAL MANAGING DIRECTOR
COLLIERS INTERNATIONAL

"Thanks again for "being" you. I really appreciate who you are and what you did with our team. It will help us immeasurably. I'm looking forward to more!"

SCOTT A. WINGET
SENIOR MANAGING DIRECTOR,
CENTER FOR WEALTH IMPACT, ASCENT

Comments

"Joel's book is an important reminder, and a corrective and alluring path forward for our turbulent, unsettling times. He's woven together profound philosophical principles and warm practical insights into an accessible method which opens up the dazzling possibility that we can invent and live a life drenched in meaning, love and contribution. Joel's fundamental goodness and unbreakable trust in life's supporting us individually in every moment shine through on every page and in every heartwarming story he tells. Here's fresh, life-giving wisdom, guidance and companionship you can take with you into every personal, relational or business situation in which you find yourself."

JAMES FLAHERTY CEO
NEW VENTURES WEST

"Self taps into something profound. There are so many people consumed by daily demands and activities, and this book illuminates the tools to see the world from a new, more meaningful, perspective. It offers each person a path to be authentic and grounded in a way that opens the door to a life they can be proud to live. With this new perspective, the past seems to move aside and the vision they can see themselves being, begins to lead them to a more productive, and meaningful life. Thank you Joel!"

JOHN YOUNGER
CHAIRMAN, HIREMOJO

"This book is a powerful voice adding to the chorus, Joel offers his unique and embodied wisdom showing us the power of our words and how we can open or close our relationships through their use. I have worked along side Joel for the last 8 years and witnessed the swiftness with which a person can change their life by shifting their words and as a result, their self. A must read for anyone wanting to experience their own brilliance, this book will show you where to look."

AMY CASTORO
CEO, THE WILLIAMS GROUP

Notes to SELF

Notes to SELF

Notes to SELF

Notes to SELF

....

....

....

....

....

....

....

....

....

....

....

....

....

Notes to SELF

Notes to SELF

Notes to SELF

Notes to SELF

Notes to SELF

Notes to SELF

CPSIA information can be obtained
at www.ICGtesting.com
Printed in the USA
BVHW02n1021020818
523326BV00001B/1/P